Kirk's Civil War Raids Along the Blue Ridge

KIRK'S CIVIL WAR RAIDS ALONG THE BLUE RIDGE

MICHAEL C. HARDY

Published by The History Press
Charleston, SC
www.historypress.net

Front cover: Union scout Dan Ellis guided many men over the mountains and into Federal lines. From *The Thrilling Adventures of Daniel Ellis*.

First published 2018

Manufactured in the United States

ISBN 9781625858467

Library of Congress Control Number: 2017960103

Contents

INTRODUCTION

"East Tennessee is my horror," William Tecumseh Sherman wrote to Ulysses S. Grant on December 1, 1863. "That any military man should send a force into East Tennessee puzzles me." For the men and women living along the North Carolina–Tennessee border in the Southern Appalachian Mountains, the war was their horror as well. There are no winners in this kind of war. For the men and women living along that border in the middle of the nineteenth century, the Civil War and its horrific aftermath became the defining epoch in their lives.[1]

The counties that make up Western North Carolina and East Tennessee are eighty-one in number. This study examines only twelve of those counties: Watauga, Ashe, Mitchell, Yancey, Madison and Haywood on the North Carolina side, and Johnson, Carter, Washington, Greene, Cocke and Sevier on the Tennessee side, including two more present-day counties carved out from that region since the end of the war, Avery and Unicoi. While the war affected every spot in the mountains of Southern Appalachia, this twelve-county corridor was the hotbed of activity for the notorious George W. Kirk and thus was the center of the whirlwind created by his actions and those of men like him.

Since most of the warfare in the mountains of North Carolina and Tennessee was unconventional in nature, sources are sparse. The accounts included here are drawn from local histories, memoirs, letters, newspaper accounts and stories passed down by descendants of participants, as well as from the official records.

Defining the various roles of the participants is a challenge. There were numerous pro-Confederate families, more so in Western North Carolina than in East Tennessee. There were also pro-Union families. Of these men, those in East Tennessee enlisted in Federal regiments as early as the opportunity presented itself. In Western North Carolina, a few Union men did choose to cross over the mountain and enlist in the Federal army. These men had quickly decided that they were not going to be conscripted into Confederate service. Then there were scores of men who waited until the last days of the war to enlist in the Union army. They realized who was going to win and most likely enlisted not out of a desire to preserve the Union or to free the slaves but in an effort to be on the winning side and therefore eligible for a later pension. In many of the letters of Confederates in Western North Carolina, there was a distinction between Unionists and Tories. This latter designation was probably for dissidents who enlisted in neither army. They might have said they were *authorized* by the Confederate or Federal governments, but they were often no more than opportunistic thieves and murderers. Finally, there were genuine, unvarnished murderers and thieves who, without even the façade of political or military motivation, used the war as an excuse to plunder their neighbors and the citizens of surrounding counties.

The conflict along the border counties was a guerrilla war in its truest form. Many used the term *guerrilla* to describe those small bands that roamed the mountain counties. These groups, according to historian David Sutherland, "decided for themselves where, when, how, and against whom to fight." Noel C. Fisher takes the definition a step further. Guerrillas "claimed no official status," engaging "in a variety of activities, including bushwhacking…assaulting and intimidating…stealing and destroying property, and occasionally raiding into neighboring states." Then there were partisans, or partisan rangers. These men were authorized by the Confederate government and were expected to obey government regulations while coordinating movements with their superiors. Sometimes the letters or stories from the war in the mountains refer to "bushwhackers." Sutherland defines bushwhackers as men who "killed people or destroyed property for sport, out of meanness, or in a personal vendetta." Many times these lines might become blurred. Men in a regular army command could be ordered into the area, usually to chase deserters or to disrupt the lines used by dissidents to cross over the mountains, only to eventually wind up living as guerrillas. A fourth group might be the dissidents themselves: people who simply wanted to sit out the war. Of the 707 confirmed deserters from the

Fifty-Eighth North Carolina Troops, a regiment made up of men from the mountains of Western North Carolina, only 135 can be documented as later joining the Federal army. The others simply hid out, pledging allegiance to neither side.[2]

The inner civil war waged along the border mountain counties had an impact on the Confederate war effort as a whole. Troops desperately needed elsewhere had to be sent into the area to protect the railroad and, after that vital infrastructure was lost in September 1863, to protect the salt and lead works in Virginia. With so many troops deployed to fight in the Army of Northern Virginia and the Army of Tennessee, many remote areas were deprived of able-bodied young men to provide for their families and to offer defense. The letters written to the men about the trying conditions back at home drove many a good soldier from the ranks. These soldiers attempted to provide for their families but were often hunted down by Confederates, Unionists and guerrillas.

Thanks for this project go out to many. Particularly invaluable assistance was provided by Judge Claude Sutton for information on Camp Vance, Michael Ledford for his fantastic research into the soldiers of the Toe River Valley, Carter County historian Scott Bowers and Tennessee historian extraordinaire Tim Massey. Like so many of my projects, this would not have been possible without the help of Elizabeth Baird Hardy. For more than twenty years, she has been willing to tramp over the mountains and hillsides, helping me track down the people of this story.

Michael C. Hardy
Crossnore, North Carolina
January 2018

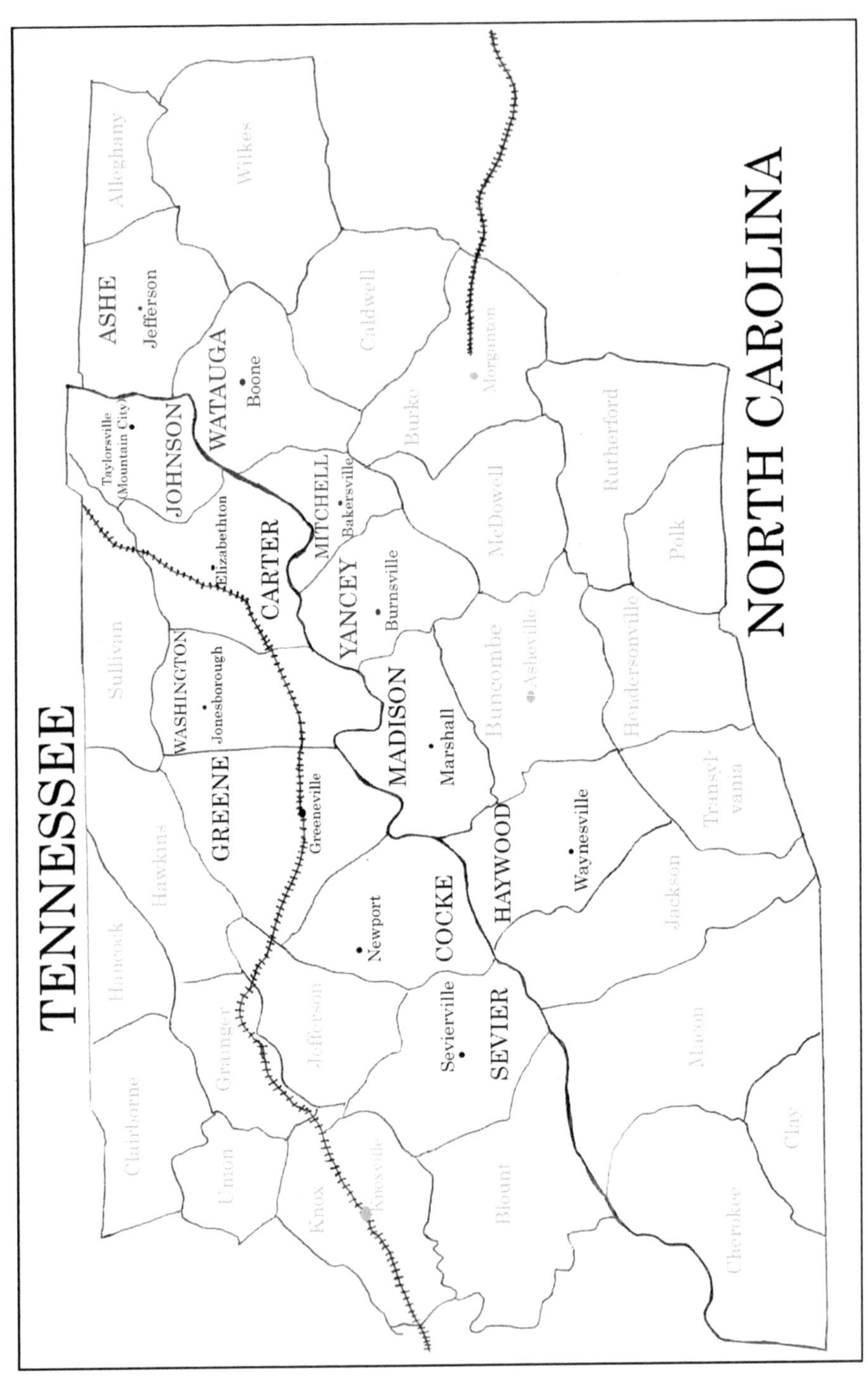

Kirk's War map.

1

1861

"We Are All Terribly Excited Here"

Marshall was ablaze with excitement. Hundreds of people had gathered in the Madison County seat to cast votes selecting delegates to the secession convention. As it did at many other nineteenth-century public gatherings, liquor flowed freely. Sheriff Ransom P. Merrill became so caught up in the day's events that he stood in the middle of town shouting, "Hurrah for Jeff Davis and the Southern Confederacy." A farmer in the crowd retorted, "George Washington and the Union." With that, Merrill drew his pistol, accusing some of those in the crowd of being "a set of dam'd black Republicans and Lincolnites." Merrill took aim at one local Unionist in the crowd and pulled the trigger. The round struck and wounded the man's son. A riot ensued, and Merrill fled to a local hotel. Merrill was pursued into the hotel by the father, who killed him.[3]

Across the mountain, events were just as heated near Jonesborough (Jonesboro during the war). As Tennessee wrestled with secession, a group in Washington County decided that if a state could leave the Union, then a district could leave a county. Citizens held a convention, passed an ordinance of secession and elected local millwright Jacob Hill as president of "Bricker's Republic," with the assistance of a congress. Representatives sent appeals to surrounding districts and counties, inviting others to join them. Bricker's Republic was short-lived. Yet there was also support for the fledging Confederacy. In neighboring Carter County, local Unionists stated that no Southern flag would be permitted in Elizabethton. Soon thereafter, Mary C. Carpenter was driving through town with a Southern flag "waving gloriously." The Unionists retreated on their promise of "shooting the flag to pieces."[4]

Geographically speaking, Western North Carolina and Eastern Tennessee share many similarities. Both are a part of the Southern Appalachian Mountains. The Appalachians run from Maine to Alabama, reaching their highest elevations in North Carolina and spreading to their greatest width in Tennessee. In both areas, settlement patterns were determined by the contours of the mountains and river valleys. All of western North Carolina is dominated by the Blue Ridge Mountains. Within the Blue Ridge are several smaller sections: the Great Smoky Mountains, the Balsams, Unakas and the Blacks. Western North Carolina and Eastern Tennessee are also connected by two main rivers: the North and South Toe Rivers form in North Carolina, becoming the Nolichucky as they enter Tennessee. The French Broad River flows through Buncombe and Madison Counties before crossing the line into Cocke County, Tennessee.

Both sections share a heritage and people. North Carolina stretched all the way to the Mississippi River until 1783, when the state ceded to Congress its western lands between the Blue Ridge Mountains and the Mississippi River. Concerns over the possible sale of the land to a foreign power led North Carolina to retract its cession, and several new counties were organized. In 1784, representatives from some of these counties declared their independence from North Carolina. They petitioned the U.S. Congress for statehood as "Franklin," in honor of Benjamin Franklin. A majority of representatives favored recognition of the State of Franklin, but the hopefuls failed to gain the required two-thirds majority. Although the State of Franklin survived until 1790, the area was marred by clashes with North Carolina officials. The State of Tennessee was organized in 1796.

While the border counties share a common history, the East Tennessee counties were far ahead of their neighboring North Carolina counties. The six North Carolina counties had an overall population of 33,276, including 1,833 slaves. The corresponding counties in East Tennessee had an overall population of 65,495, including 3,716 slaves. Other than a few iron and copper mines, the Western North Carolina border counties had no industry, and the economy primarily consisted of small farms and subsistence farmers. The closest railroad terminated six miles east of Morganton, in Burke County. From Burnsville, in Yancey County, it was forty-five miles to the railhead. The lack of good roads made the trip one of several days. A much better route, the Old Buncombe Turnpike, passed through Madison County, connecting the rich East Tennessee farmland with markets farther south.

Tennessee was fortunate to have the East Tennessee and Virginia Railroad, chartered in 1848, running from Bristol to Knoxville. The line passed through Jonesborough, Blountville and Greeneville, with several other stops along the way. Access to a railroad brought expanded opportunities and growth. Greeneville had at least six stores, four hotels, two photographers, boot and shoe makers and carriage and wagon makers, along with a cotton dealer and bookseller. Carter and Johnson Counties boasted several iron mines.[5]

Like much of their respective states, the border area was torn asunder by the sectional crisis of the 1860s. Some citizens favored secession outright. A public debate at Washington College, near Jonesborough, occurred in the fall of 1860. Henry M. Doak, great-grandson of Reverend Samuel Doak, who had preached a legendary sermon to the Overmountain Men before their historic journey to Kings Mountain in 1780, declared himself for secession from the North. The college president was opposed to disunion and encouraged Doak to "suppress" his beliefs. At a political rally in Asheville, Burke County resident Burgess Gaither called himself an "unconditional Unionist," opposed to the idea of any state trying to leave the Union.[6]

There were three candidates on the 1860 presidential ballot in North Carolina and Tennessee. Two were Democrats. Vice President John Breckinridge represented the Southern Democrats, while Stephen Douglas was chosen by the Northern branch of the party. A third nominee was on the ballot: John Bell represented the Constitutional Union Party. In the South, the contest was between Breckinridge and Bell. Breckinridge was seen as upholding the rights of the South "and the equality of the States," and he was willing to "defend the rights of Southern men against the aggressions of Northern fanatics." Bell and the Constitutional Union Party saw the preservation of the Union as their primary goal. Breckinridge carried North Carolina by 3,700 votes, while Bell won Tennessee by a little more than 4,600 votes. The border counties were equally divided. Four of the six Tennessee counties voted for Bell, while the other two went to Breckinridge. In North Carolina, Madison County's votes were voided, while Haywood and Yancey went for Breckinridge, and Ashe and Watauga supported Bell.[7]

Neither Breckinridge nor Bell won the election. Abraham Lincoln, a Republican from Illinois, had the distinction of being the first person from his party to become president of the United States. Because of the platform of the Republican Party, many in the Deep South moved to secede from the Union. South Carolina voted to leave in December 1860, followed by Mississippi, Florida, Georgia, Louisiana and Texas. Representatives from these states met in Montgomery, Alabama, in February and created the Confederate States of America. There were cries for the other Southern states to join those of the Deep South. Both North Carolina and Tennessee adopted "wait and see" attitudes.

Politicians called for state conventions to consider whether their states should leave the Union. Often, communities held competing debates. In Yancey County, there was a resolution passed against secession in December 1860. A couple of weeks later, two Buncombe County politicians, David Coleman and Bayles Edney, were in Burnsville speaking for secession. At the latter, Zebulon Baird Vance, the United States congressman for the Tenth District, was hanged in effigy for his strong pro-Union stance. There were likewise two meetings held in Buncombe County in early January 1861, one for and one against secession. Western North Carolina was caught between the pro-Union stance of many in East Tennessee and South Carolina's radicals. One Unionist was quoted as proclaiming, "For God's sake! Let South Carolina nullify, revolute, secede, and BE DAMNED!"[8]

On January 29, the North Carolina General Assembly passed legislation that set voters to cast ballots on February 28 on the question of calling a convention, while at the same time electing 120 delegates if the idea of calling a convention passed. Almost every county had a slate of representatives running in support and one running in opposition. In Watauga County, John B. Palmer, who had recently moved from Michigan and settled along the Linville River, chronicled right after the war that in 1861, he "became a candidate…for a State Convention and in campaigning…took strong and decided grounds against secession and counseled the people to vote against the convention scheme." In Yancey County, which included the recently formed Mitchell County, Milton Penland, the wealthiest man in the Toe River region, ran against fellow slave owner and Unionist G.W. Garland.[9]

When the votes were tallied, North Carolina had, by 650 votes, declined to call a convention. Ashe (with the recently formed Alleghany County) and Watauga voted overwhelmingly not to call a convention. Madison was 60 percent opposed to calling a convention. Yancey and Mitchell were just barely against calling a convention, while Haywood was over 60 percent in favor of the convention. For a short amount of time, the Unionist elements of the state, along with those advising the wait and see approach, were able to keep North Carolina in the Union.[10]

The debates were equally heated in Eastern Tennessee. Knoxville lawyer Oliver P. Temple spoke to a group of one thousand Unionists in Sevier County in January 1861. Temple recalled that these "were not learned men,

A group of Unionists meeting and pledging to remain loyal to the Union. *From* Harper's Weekly.

but they had a simple, pure, unswerving love of country. They had learned by traditions handed down from father to son, of the great Revolutionary struggle for independence.…[T]he Republic was therefore as dear to them as was the Sacred Ark of the Covenant to the Israelites." A meeting on January 28, "irrespective of parties," was held in Jonesborough. Pro-Union resolutions were adopted. Following this, Democrats called for a second meeting, in which pro-Southern resolutions were adopted. Gatlinburg resident Richard Gatlin was run out of the town that bears his name for his pro-secession beliefs. The congregation of the church barred him from preaching and then burned his barns. In Greeneville, a "Palmetto flag" floated in town, but it was soon hauled down. Senator Andrew Johnson was hanged in effigy in Memphis and Knoxville and then at Tusculum College near Greeneville. William G. Brownlow, editor of the *Knoxville Whig*, considered all of the secession ordinances emerging from the Deep South "covenants with death and agreements with hell."[11]

Governor Isham G. Harris convened a special session of the Tennessee General Assembly on January 7 to discuss the current events. At first, Harris proposed to send a compromise plan to the other Southern states. All of Harris's proposals concerned the slavery issue. He confessed, however, that he had little faith in a compromise and believed the real question concerned Tennessee's allegiance. Harris then called for the passage of an ordinance of secession. However, the politicians hesitated, instead authorizing a referendum on secession for February 9. As with the balloting in North Carolina, voters in Tennessee elected delegates just in case the call for a convention passed. All of the border counties voted against calling a convention, and overall, the measure was defeated 68,282 to 59,449. One Knoxville merchant was heard to call his city "a d----d Abolition hole, and as far as South of our river, it was a *puke* of an abolition hole."[12]

Opinions were already shifting by early March. Congressional attempts to reach a compromise had failed, and in late February, the delegates to the Washington Peace Conference returned, after also failing to achieve a conclusion. Had news regarding the failure of the conference reached the Western North Carolina counties a day earlier, it might have swung the vote toward secession. Lincoln's inaugural address further unsettled many. It sounded conciliatory, affirming that there would be no invasion and no bloodshed, unless the United States government was forced into action. However, Lincoln's speech failed to console either Unionists or Secessionists. In early April came the attack on Fort Sumter in Charleston, South Carolina. Lincoln then issued a call for seventy-five thousand volunteers to go into the Deep South states to crush the rebellion. Both North Carolina's and Tennessee's governors had the same answer: Lincoln would get no troops from their states.[13]

Just as caught up in the excitement were the border counties. A pro-Confederate rally in Yancey County featured a brass band. "[A]ll turned out for the South" at a rally in Madison County.

Right: William G. Brownlow, sometimes known as Parson Brownlow, was a newspaper editor, minister and politician. He was forced to flee East Tennessee early in the war but, in January 1865, was elected governor. *Library of Congress.*

Below: Tusculum College, near Greeneville, was the site of several early debates about secession. *Author's collection.*

Congressman Zebulon B. Vance was in the midst of a pro-Union rally when word arrived of the attack on Fort Sumter. After the war, he recalled the scene:

> *I was addressing a large and excited crowd, large numbers of whom were armed, and literally had my arm extended upward in pleading for peace and the Union of our Fathers, when the telegraphic news was announced of the firing on Sumter and the President's call for seventy-five thousand volunteers. When my hand came down from that impassioned gesticulation, it fell slowly and sadly by the side of a secessionist. I immediately, with altered voice and manner, called upon the assembled multitude to volunteer, not to fight against but for South Carolina.*

Volunteers began forming for state and Confederate service. Three days after Lincoln's demand for troops, two companies from Burke and Buncombe Counties volunteered for state service. They were soon en route to Raleigh to become members of the First North Carolina Cavalry. Harvey Davis recorded a rally in Watauga County in early May: "After a somewhat firey speech by G.N. Folk…in which the speaker dwelt at large on the attempt of the North to dominate the South and abrogate her rights under the Constitution, a call was made for volunteers.…It seemed as if the whole assembly of citizens soon were in line." Davis's company became a part of the First North Carolina Cavalry.[14]

Tar Heel governor John Ellis ordered a special meeting of the North Carolina General Assembly on May 1. The participants called for the election of 120 delegates on May 13 and then a convention to meet in Raleigh on May 20. In most counties in North Carolina, there were no clearly defined parties, with many of the secessionist candidates running unopposed. The group that met on May 20 has been considered "one of the ablest political bodies ever assembled in North Carolina." An ordinance of secession was unanimously adopted to the peals of bells and cannons. After passing the ordinance of secession, the delegates then ratified the provisional constitution of the Confederate States of America, at the same time defeating a motion that ratification of the document should be placed before the people. On May 21, all 120 delegates signed the secession ordinance.

There were, of course, dissenters. The Election Day violence in Madison County, in which the sheriff lost his life, was not an isolated occurrence. There was also violence in Henderson County. However, in Western North Carolina, Unionists retreated to their own homes while thousands of mountaineers poured forth to fight for the Confederacy. Each of the six border counties had organized a company of volunteers for Confederate service, and Ashe had produced a second company before North Carolina formally left the Union on May 20, 1861.

In East Tennessee, the debate was even more virulent. An alliance between the old Whigs and Democrats began to disintegrate. Many were upset over the way patronage was doled out by the Lincoln administration. Lincoln passed some of the responsibility on to Andrew Johnson, who promptly nominated a secessionist as district attorney for East Tennessee. There were pro-Union meetings in Carter, Johnson and Greene Counties in April. There was even a proposal that Carter and Johnson Counties should secede from Tennessee and form their own Confederacy, with Andrew Johnson president and T.A.R. Nelson vice president. Yet in those same counties were many in favor of secession. "[W]e are all terribly excited here, a complete revolution has taken place in public sentiment nearly all are for separation and resistance. Many of the Union men are for immediate secession," one Jonesborough resident wrote on May 1. Two weeks later, a Carter County resident told a Knoxville newspaper that the "fire of Southern Independence is spread here." They had held a pro-Confederate meeting, complete with a flag, martial music, a procession of ladies and speeches by Godfrey C. Nave, William J. Stover and Dr. S.M. Stover. A company of "Minute men for home protection" was raised, "and giving three cheers for Southern Independence, we adjourned."[15]

Governor Harris, on April 15, called for a meeting of the legislature in Nashville. The Tennessee General Assembly convened on April 25, and much of the next two weeks was held in secret session. On May 6, the legislators passed a Declaration of Independence, submitting it to the people in a referendum scheduled for June 8. The action of the assembly was considered tantamount to secession. Governor Harris informed the legislators on May 7 that he had agreed to a military allegiance between the state and the Confederate government, an action they approved. Joining North Carolina and Tennessee were other Upper South states of Virginia and Arkansas.

Many of the Unionists in East Tennessee were not going to abandon the Union willingly. On May 30–31, over 450 Unionists from twenty-nine Tennessee counties met in a grove outside Temperance Hall in Knoxville. Some of these men were elected at local rallies, while others were self-appointed. Resolutions affirming loyalty to the Union and illegality of secession were passed to the approval of the attendees. After speeches by

Isham Harris led the push for Tennessee to leave the Union. *Library of Congress.*

Andrew Johnson and T.A.R. Nelson, the group agreed to reassemble in Greeneville following the June 8 referendum.

Campaigning in East Tennessee between May 7 and June 8 was unlike any previous campaigns. In Carter, Johnson and the surrounding counties, Unionists threatened violence against anyone voting for secession. American flags were flying in Greeneville, and a brass band was heard playing "The Star-Spangled Banner." In Elizabethton, Johnson used biblical allusions in his speech, claiming secession was like the expulsion of Adam and Eve from the Garden of Eden. After eating the fruit, they "seceded and retired from the enjoyments that had been placed before them in Paradise." After Judas betrayed Christ, "he also seceded to put an end to his existence." In Jonesborough, the crowd booed and cursed Johnson, calling him a "*God Damned Traitor*—told him that he was hired by Lincoln to make speeches....When he went to start out to Nelson's they raised the shout, groaned and *booed* him out of Town....You never seen such a time[,] men on horses whipping up and down the street screaming upon the tops of their voices *you damned Traitor you damned Traitor.*" Rain forced the meeting indoors, where Johnson and Nelson were finally able to deliver their remarks. While the Unionists were in transit to Nelson's home later, they saw secession flags hanging from the windows and were jeered by local citizens.[16]

Tennessee confirmed its earlier vote to join the Southern Confederacy on June 8. Once the referendum votes were tallied, 102,172 to 47,238 voted in favor of leaving. Unionists in East Tennessee were stunned. Even in their bastion of Unionist support, the voting majority dropped from 80 percent to 69 percent. At this point, some East Tennessee Unionists chose to flee the state. Andrew Johnson departed Greeneville on June 12, heading to Washington, D.C. On June 17, a smaller group of Unionists met at the Greene County Courthouse. This group split into two factions. The Radicals issued a Declaration of Grievances, writing that Tennessee's Declaration of Independence was unconstitutional and that the Unionist counties in East and Middle Tennessee now constituted the real State of Tennessee. They would remain neutral, like Kentucky, but if invaded by Confederate forces, they would resist, call upon the Federal government for protection and retaliate against their Confederate neighbors. Unionists in surrounding counties were encouraged to arm themselves and raise companies for self-defense. Conservative members of the Greeneville Convention believed that these resolutions would hasten Confederate occupation. A series of moderate resolutions was submitted and, after several days of heated debate, adopted. It was agreed that three representatives would be sent to Nashville, seeking consent for the eastern counties of Tennessee to be granted permission to establish a separate state. After four days, the meeting adjourned.[17]

Even as the delegates met, Confederate soldiers were passing through Greeneville. On June 18, the Louisiana Tigers arrived in town, traveling to Manassas. These colorful men were recruited from the wharfs and docks in New Orleans, and their officers frequently had trouble controlling them. A group of Tigers consumed the breakfasts of several of the delegates at a local hotel and then cut down a United States flag near the courthouse

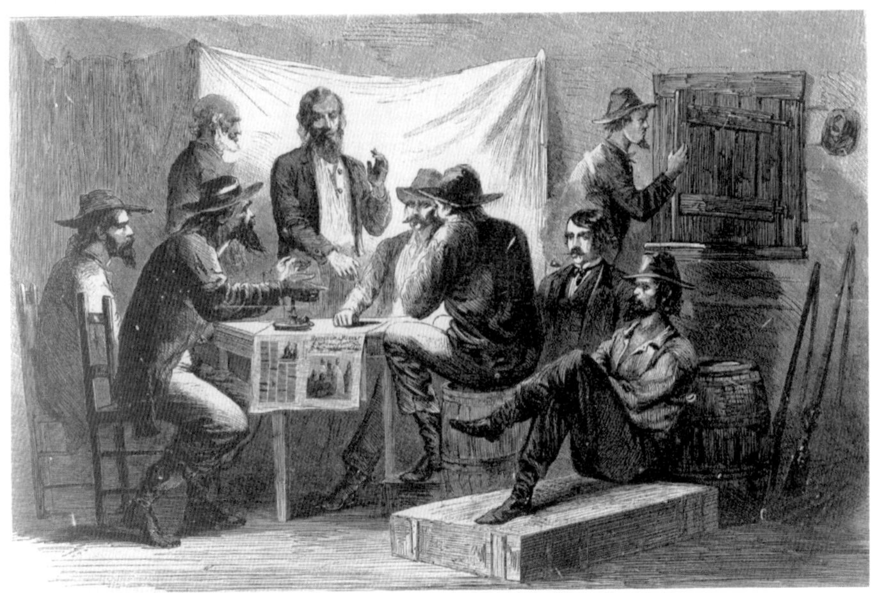

Famed artist Alfred Waud penned this sketch of East Tennessee Unionists secretly meeting. *Library of Congress.*

where the conventioneers were meeting, threatening several delegates at the same time. The Unionists were probably relieved that the Louisiana soldiers were soon back on the train, headed to Virginia.[18]

East Tennessee men were also organizing and enlisting for Confederate service. In Jonesborough, a company of volunteers paraded through town, listening to speeches and bearing the motto "Resistance" on the left breast of their uniforms. A Knoxville newspaper reported that Washington County had three companies mustered by May 18. One of those belonged to Zadock Willett, a cadet at the United States Military Academy at West Point prior to the secession crisis. By the time Tennessee secession was ratified by the people, two of these companies were enrolled in Confederate service.[19]

Volunteers continued to pour out of the mountains of Western North Carolina throughout the summer and fall months. By the end of 1861, the border counties had sent nineteen companies into Confederate service, some 1,900 men. Likewise, the Tennessee border counties sent thirteen companies, about 1,300 men, into the Confederate ranks during the same time. The only county out of the twelve that did not put a company into Confederate service was Johnson County.

Many of the same motivating factors that pushed men from the Deep South states into the Confederate army also factored into the decisions of men in Western North Carolina and Eastern Tennessee. These soldiers enlisted because their fathers and grandfathers were Patriots during the American Revolution, fighting for freedom from a tyrannical government. With popular opinion holding that the war would last just three months, with one big battle to prove the winner, many volunteered out of a sense of adventure. A few undoubtedly enlisted out of fear of the Radical Republican plans, which included preventing slavery from spreading into the territories and passing tariffs protecting Northern industry. Those voices are strangely silent from the historical records along the border counties. The vast majority were instead motivated by the atmosphere in the communities where they lived. An Ashe County church resolution, written in October 1861, probably summed up the attitudes for most early enlistees:

> *Where as our Country is involved in a revolutionary war, the North against the South of the unjust savage caractor* [character] *the North having denied the South her constitutional guarantees, not withstanding peaceful overtures, was made by the South and called on the North again and again to settle the difficulties by Equitable negotiations to prevent the resort to the sacrifice of human life, all was proudly denied and nothing was left the South but stern resistance on abject submission to unconstitutional power, and so on.*[20]

Despite the rush of men to fight under the Confederate flag, homogenous support was far from reality. There were many rumors of incursions and acts of disloyalty, at least to the Confederates. William "Bull" Nelson, an officer in the U.S. Navy, was ordered by Lincoln to East Tennessee to raise a regiment of cavalry in July 1861. It was reported in August that Reverend Nathaniel G. Taylor, who had spoken out in defense of the Union during the 1860 presidential campaign, had fled to the Crab Orchard section of Carter County. He was guarded by 100 fellow mountaineers. Taylor promised that any attempted movements by Confederate troops would be met with force. Southern troops "would have to march over his dead body and the dead bodies of thousands of East Tennessee mountaineers slain in battle." There were reports of 1,800 Unionists drilling in Greene County and of Unionists in Johnson and Carter Counties killing 2 local secessionists and wounding several others. The pro-Confederate clerk in Johnson County was forced to resign, fleeing the state.[21]

That unrest might have spilled over the North Carolina border. It was reported in August that East Tennessee Tories raided Watauga County, "abducting several citizens" and holding "the persons taken as hostages for the safety of Nelson." T.A.R. Nelson was elected for a second term in Congress in 1861 and was on his way to take his seat in Washington, D.C., when he was arrested and imprisoned in Richmond. A couple of weeks later came a widely published newspaper report of a group of "Fifty hundred Tennesseeans and Wataugans" crossing over into Watauga County "trying to arouse those people against the Southern movements." Cavalry was dispatched to the area "to bring them back." It was the advice of the newspaper that North Carolina should "be on her guard, and let her authorities hang or shoot every tory and Yankee they may lay their hands upon. If they make any more demonstrations in Watauga, the farmers should rise en masse to suppress them." The *Raleigh Standard* transmitted more information on the mobs that roamed through Tennessee, adding "that the militia of Ashe, Watauga and other counties on the western line" of North Carolina "turned out in such numbers to meet the Lincolnites of East Tennessee." There is probably some validity to the newspaper articles. Barzilla McBride, serving in the First North Carolina Cavalry, wrote home on August 25, 1861: "I was sorry to hear that them tories was creating so much excitement if our Regiment was up there in N.C. we could soon clear them out."[22]

Politicians wrote back and forth about the importance of the area, especially East Tennessee and its railroad. Landon Carter Haynes, who later became a Confederate senator, wrote to Confederate secretary of war Leroy P. Walker in July 1861 about his concerns. He noted reports of Unionists in the area and mentioned weapons coming through Tennessee. Haynes quoted articles from New York and Kentucky newspapers, stating, "East Tennessee is a vital point to the Lincoln Government." Local men were encouraged to seize and hold Knoxville. Haynes was surprised that the bridges of the East Tennessee and Virginia Railroad were still standing and believed that a guard needed to be sent to the area. At the same time in Washington, D.C., Lincoln was coping with the debacle known as the Battle of First Manassas. Over the course of two different days, he outlined a grand strategy for the Union war effort. The last point of the eleven in the plan proposed that after Federal forces seized Manassas and Strasburg, two joint movements should take place. One was from Cairo to Memphis, while the other was from Cincinnati and into East Tennessee. General George B. McClellan, commanding in the Ohio Valley area, wrote that if the United

States government would supply him ten thousand muskets, he could march into East Tennessee and "break the backbone of secession."[23]

Lincoln's grand strategy, at least concerning East Tennessee, was soon to play out rather miserably. On July 26, 1861, Brigadier General Felix K. Zollicoffer was assigned to command Confederate troops in East Tennessee. Zollicoffer found an area rife with discontent. "[T]here are very many Lincoln men here will be restrained from cooperating [with a Union invasion] only by consideration of policy or apprehension of the circumstances," he wrote on August 6. Zollicoffer wanted to deal gently with local Unionists, trying to preserve harmony in East Tennessee. A week later, he wrote the War Department that fourteen thousand Confederate troops were needed to "crush out [the] rebellion there [East Tennessee] without firing a gun." This was undoubtedly disheartening news to officials in Richmond. It had taken a force of thirty-two thousand troops to defeat the Federals at Manassas a month earlier.[24]

The Confederate government did not have fourteen thousand soldiers to send to Zollicoffer. There were countless regiments traveling through the area via the railroad, bound for Virginia, but he only had a couple of regiments at his disposal. The Fourteenth Mississippi Infantry, along with a company of cavalry, was ordered on August 26 to Fish Springs, on the border of Johnson and Carter Counties. Colonel William Baldwin was provided a list of "Lincoln leaders" in the two counties and had orders to "disarm and disperse all bodies of men in open hostility to the authorities… capture and hold their leaders, and if resistance is offered…destroy them." Baldwin's orders allowed him to move freely in the area, as circumstances warranted. The Fourteenth Mississippi remained until early September, when the regiment was ordered toward Kentucky.[25]

At the same time, Greene County Unionist David Fry was reportedly "drilling companies under the Stars and Stripes…and threatening death to Southern Rights men." A company of Confederates under Captain James Fry, stationed a few miles away at Midway, was ordered to arrest the Unionists. Several of them were apprehended, when, according to the newspaper, a party of fifty Unionists attacked a group of twelve or fifteen Confederates on Cedar Creek. One of the Confederates was killed before the skirmish ended. The Confederate Captain Fry was spotted in Greeneville a few days later, with several Unionists in tow.[26]

Part of the job of the Confederate soldiers stationed in East Tennessee was to prevent local citizens from slipping over the mountain and joining Federal regiments organizing in Kentucky. After William Polk lost the gubernatorial race to Isham Harris in the general election in August 1861, hundreds of young men began heading to Kentucky. At Camp Dick Robinson, both the First and Second East Tennessee Infantry Regiments (U.S.) were organized in September 1861. One of those who escaped across the lines was Reverend William B. Carter, a retired Presbyterian minister living in Carter County and one of the most active Unionists in the area. According to a later biographical sketch, Carter concocted the idea of a simultaneous raid on the railroad bridges running through East Tennessee. At Camp Dick Robinson, Carter met with General William T. Sherman, Andrew Johnson, Horace Maynard and General George H. Thomas. Also present was William Carter's brother, Samuel Carter, an officer in the U.S. Navy whom Lincoln had sent to organize Tennessee forces in Kentucky. Reverend Carter's plan was discussed, and only Sherman remained unconvinced of its plausibility. Thomas eventually persuaded Sherman to back the plot. William Carter journeyed to Washington, D.C., and met with Lincoln, Federal army commander George McClellan and Secretary of State William Seward. Carter proposed the destruction of nine railroad bridges between Bridgeport, Alabama, and Bristol on the Tennessee-Virginia border. Once this infrastructure was destroyed, a Federal force could advance from Cumberland Gap to Knoxville, capturing the rail connection there. Then, East Tennessee Unionists could organize themselves into fighting forces to help secure the area. All three approved the plan, and Carter was soon on his way back to Kentucky with $2,500 to help finance the operation.[27]

Carter set out with two officers, including Greene County's Captain David Fry, in mid-October. Their goal was to recruit local leaders who, in turn, would enlist others to carry out the bridge-burning mission. Frequently, Carter sent updates to Thomas. On October 22, he was near Montgomery County, Tennessee. Five days later, he was close to Kingston. While there, he believed that if he could recruit enough men to "take the bull by the horns," then the small bands of Confederate cavalry he encountered could be whipped, and the bridges could be spared. Carter had heard that Confederate commanders were "uneasy" and had asked Richmond for reinforcements but were told that there were no troops to spare. Zollicoffer had moved into Kentucky in September, but his force was defeated at the Battle of Wildcat Mountain in late October. Thomas was moving toward Cumberland Gap, the staging area for the movement against Knoxville. Yet Sherman was backtracking in his support of the operation.[28]

Zollicoffer was aware of the massing Federal soldiers in Kentucky. He wrote on October 29 of nine thousand Federal soldiers stationed on the

Samuel P. Carter was the only officer during the war to be commissioned as both an admiral in the U.S. Navy and a general in the U.S. Army. The idea for a mass bridge burning in East Tennessee was his. *Library of Congress.*

Rockcastle River. On November 4, he informed Richmond of not only that nine thousand but also another ten thousand between Camp Dick Robinson and Cincinnati. Zollicoffer planned to mass his men at Cumberland Gap to block the passage of the Federals.[29]

The raid against the railroad was scheduled for the night of November 8. Thomas wrote Sherman on November 5: "With my headquarters at Somerset [Kentucky] I can easily seize the most favorable time for invading East Tennessee." At the same time, Thomas wrote to Andrew Johnson: "I have done all in my power to get troops and transportation and means to advance into Tennessee....Up to this time we have been unsuccessful. If the Tennesseans are not content and must go, then the risk of disaster will remain with them." Sherman replied to Thomas, not doubting the importance of the movement, but confessing that he had not the troops, nor the transportation, to support the operation. While Sherman did not specifically tell Thomas to abandon the expedition, his letter was enough to dissuade any support.[30]

All of the missives passing between Sherman and Thomas were unknown to Carter. He still believed that Federal forces would soon be pouring through the gaps in the Cumberland Mountains to liberate East Tennessee. Different parties of men crept toward their targets on the night of November 8. William C. Pickens led his twelve raiders from Sevier County to the bridge at Strawberry Plains on the Knox-Jefferson County border. After a struggle in the darkness with the lone guard, who managed to escape, the saboteurs discovered that their matches had fallen into the Holston River, and the plan was aborted. Pickens was wounded in the mêlée.[31]

To the northeast, David Fry led his group of almost sixty men to the bridge over the Lick Creek in Greene County. Six guards were captured, the telegraph was cut and the bridge was soon in flames. Farther north, the son-in-law of Andrew Johnson, Daniel Stover, led a group toward the bridge over the Watauga River at Carter's Depot. Encountering an entire company of Confederate soldiers, Stover retreated into the darkness. He and his men moved ten miles to the bridge over the Holston River in present-day Bluff City, Sullivan County, captured the two guards and soon left the bridge in charred ruins. After swearing they would not reveal the bridge burners' identities, the two guards were released unharmed. Stover's party then returned to the Carter's Depot bridge and, in the darkness, skirmished with Captain David McClellan's independent cavalry company. Stover was not able to overpower these Confederates and retreated. In all, five bridges were destroyed.[32]

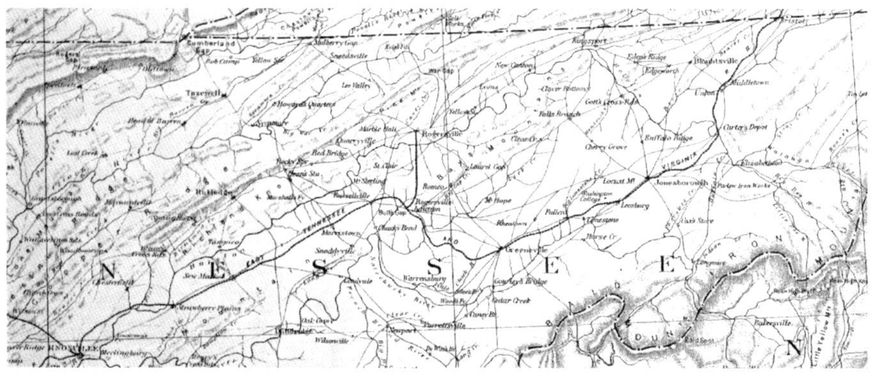

The East Tennessee and Virginia Railroad witnessed much of the war, from the bridge burnings in November 1861 to repeated attacks through 1864. *Library of Congress.*

Using the bridge burnings as a signal, local Unionists began to rally. In Sevier County, four hundred men moved toward Strawberry Plains. At Underdowns Ferry on the French Broad River in Sevier County, they encountered a Confederate force, and a thirty-six-hour skirmish ensued before the Unionists retreated. After the burning of the bridge in Sullivan County, Daniel Stover led his men back toward Elizabethton. Like those in Sevier County, Unionists flocked to Elizabethton from the surrounding counties. According to one postwar account, there were one thousand men gathering at Sycamore Shoals, some armed. They organized themselves by electing officers. Pickets were posted toward Carter's Depot.[33]

Response from Confederate officials came swiftly. Secretary of War Judah P. Benjamin published an order authorizing those who were identified as bridge burners, when captured, to be "tried summarily by drum-head court-martial, and, if found guilty, executed on the spot by hanging." Any other Unionists captured were to be treated as prisoners of war and sent to Tuscaloosa, Alabama. Weapons found were to be seized. If a Unionist came in voluntarily, surrendering his weapons and taking the Oath of Allegiance, he could be treated with leniency. A "mild or conciliating policy will do no good; they [Unionists] must be punished to the extent of the law. Nothing short of this will give quiet to the country," Colonel Wood wrote to Richmond. General Zollicoffer also changed his views, believing that Unionist leaders should be seized and imprisoned.[34]

At the same time, Richmond appointed the acting chief of the Engineering Bureau, Danville Leadbetter, to the temporary rank of colonel on November 9 and ordered him on November 11 to East Tennessee. He was assigned command of all troops between Bristol and Chattanooga. Leadbetter was in the area by November 15, when it was reported that he arrived at Johnson's Depot with "a large force and two mountain howitzers." He pushed toward the Unionists in Carter County. There was minor skirmishing between the two sides, and the Confederate advance was pushed back. Realizing that they were up against a large force, the Unionists broke camp at Elizabethton and, according to one of their number, retreated three miles to "the Big Spring, on Gap Creek." Leadbetter's force moved into Elizabethton the next day, scouring the area for Unionists. The group gathered on Gap Creek retreated farther south into the Doe River Cove area. Leadbetter soon followed, and the Unionists were forced to flee deeper into the mountains, hiding in the hollows, caves, laurel hells and cedar thickets. Leadbetter remained in the area for several days and, on taking his leave, burned the remnants of the Unionists' shanties. At least twenty-one men were taken prisoner and forwarded to Knoxville.[35]

Having disrupted the Unionist camp in Carter County, Leadbetter pulled out his troops and headed west. Reports arrived of a Unionist group numbering two to three hundred at Chimney Top, on the Greene-Hawkins County line. Leadbetter was unable to catch up to the faction, but reports also arrived of "insurgents" heading for Cocke and Sevier Counties. On November 24, the Unionists were reported near Parrottsville. As the Confederates continued to sweep the area, they were able to capture three of the alleged bridge-burners: Henry Fry, Jacob Hishaw and Hugh Self. On December 3, Leadbetter moved with the Twenty-Ninth North Carolina Troops and two companies of the Third Georgia Battalion toward Parrottsville. Leadbetter was working with at least part of a force under Brigadier General William H. Carroll, a force that included the Twenty-Ninth Tennessee Infantry. Some dissidents were seen early in the expedition, but after exchanging a few shots, they disappeared into the mountains. "The women in some cases were greatly alarmed," Leadbetter wrote, "throwing themselves on the ground and wailing like savages." The "population is savage," he concluded. A part of Carroll's force crossed the Chucky River and shelled Unionists on Bird Hill. One newspaper reported another thirty-one men captured or arrested. Confederate losses are really unknown. Captain Thomas Gorman, Fifth Tennessee Cavalry, was wounded. Two other Confederates were reportedly killed.[36]

Leadbetter pulled the bulk of his force out of the mountains, setting up his headquarters in Greeneville. However, three companies of the Twenty-Ninth North Carolina Troops were left at Parrottsville and three at Warrensburg,

Greene County, with orders to capture "troublesome men" and "impress horses from Union men" in the area. They were also ordered to requisition provisions, giving certificates for payment. "The whole country is given to understand that this course will be pursued until quiet shall be restored.... [N]o prisoner will be pardoned so long as any Union men shall remain in arms," Leadbetter told his superiors. Leadbetter's arrival and subsequent actions marked a sharp shift in Confederate policy toward East Tennessee Unionists. They were coming in to take the oath and surrendering arms. "It is believed that we are making progress towards pacification," Leadbetter wrote. He even went so far as to issue a proclamation to the citizens of East Tennessee. Submission to Confederate authority was better than resistance, Leadbetter wrote, "[s]o long as you are up in arms against these States can you look for anything but the invasion of your homes and the wasting of your substance."[37]

The exact number of men involved in the East Tennessee bridge-burning campaign will never be known. Some estimates place the number around one hundred men total, while others project upward of three hundred. Of that number, at least eight were captured and five hanged. The first drumhead courts-martial appear to be for Henry Fry and Jacob Hishaw. After being found guilty on November 30, they were hanged from an oak tree

Henry Fry and Jacob Hishaw were the first two of the bridge burners to hang. *From* Sketches of the Rise, Progress, and Decline of Secession.

An artist's conception of the execution of Jacob Harmon and his son. According to the historical record, Jacob watched his son's hanging shortly before his own. *From* Sketches of the Rise, Progress, and Decline of Secession.

near the railroad depot. Their bodies were left for passersby to observe for twenty-four hours before being taken down and buried. The others were taken to Knoxville to face charges. Christopher A. Haun was tried, found guilty and hanged on December 10 or possibly December 11. The *Knoxville Register* reported that Haun confessed on the scaffolding that he had been a bridge burner and, given the chance, "would do it again." Jacob Harmon and his son Thomas were tried in Knoxville and found guilty. According to a fellow Knoxville prisoner, a cart came and took the pair to the gallows. Jacob was forced to sit and watch his son's execution. After the deed was done, the father, "overpowered by his feeling," stumbled. "Get up there, you damned old traitor!" one of the guards barked as they pulled Jacob up onto the gallows and executed him. Harrison Self was tried next and found guilty. According to one postwar source, his daughter arrived before the execution and, after spending time with her imprisoned father, sent a telegram to Jefferson Davis, asking for a stay of execution. Others wrote on behalf of Self, claiming that he had tried to persuade the others not to burn the bridges and, in the end, was "dragged into participation in it." Self's execution was stayed.[38]

David Fry initially was wounded and captured in March 1862 while trying to escape to Kentucky. He was imprisoned in Georgia, but he later escaped. Two others, David Smith and Jacob Myers, were found guilty and sent to a prison in Tuscaloosa, Alabama. Many of the political prisoners from East Tennessee were also sent to Tuscaloosa.[39]

For everyone along the border counties between North Carolina and Tennessee, 1861 had been a divisive year. Families were literally torn asunder, while neighborhoods and communities likewise were forced to choose sides in a war that few wanted. There was bloodshed in early 1861, but the burning of bridges in East Tennessee in November brought the war home. Confederate forces moved into the area in force, and many citizens became outliers in their own communities. Across the line in North Carolina, thousands of young men poured forth to join Confederate regiments, regiments that often headed east, leaving family members unprotected and managing farms in their absence. Everyone was anxious to see what 1862 would bring.

2

1862

"This County Is a Perfect Den of Thieves and Tories"

The East Tennessee bridge burnings alarmed many North Carolinians. Newspapers in New Bern, Raleigh, Fayetteville and even Wilmington ran stories about the events. It was also widely reported that many of the bridge burners and other dissidents had escaped across the state line to Madison County. The *Asheville News* estimated the number to be between two and three hundred men in the area. Some newspaper editors wanted to debunk such notions, but the problem was serious enough that the citizens of Yancey County met and passed resolutions, imploring the local militia colonel, John W. McElroy, to call out his men to protect the populace.[40]

Officials in Raleigh went even further to address the possible threat. The Twenty-Ninth Regiment was moved into East Tennessee, while Major David Coleman's battalion of five companies went into position five miles north of Asheville at Camp Hill. At the same time, Governor Henry Clark, who had replaced Governor Ellis after he died in office, authorized the formation of ranger companies in the counties that bordered East Tennessee. Their job was to protect "citizens against incursions from abroad." Colonel McElroy was charged with raising a company in Yancey County. Dr. Joseph A. McDowell directed the ranger company in Madison County. Haywood County postmaster Robert H. Penland was responsible for that county, while William H. Thomas was in charge of the Jackson County company. The responsibility fell on John B. Palmer in the newly formed Mitchell County. Palmer was probably the first to begin his recruiting, organizing the Mitchell

Rangers on December 31, 1861. This company was a mixed infantry and cavalry company, at times also known as Palmer's Legion. Many of his men came from the upper Linville River area, present-day lower Avery County. Palmer was originally from Plattsburg, New York. After the death of his father, a two-term congressman, he moved to Detroit, Michigan, and then to the Linville River area in 1858. He was one of the wealthiest non–slave owning men in Western North Carolina. His wife, Frances Marvin Kirby, was a cousin to Confederate general Edmund Kirby Smith. A few counties southwest, William H. Thomas met with Cherokee Indians in Quallatown on January 3 and 4 and began organizing his company. Thomas had grown up at a trading post in Soco Creek. He had been adopted by a local family and had learned to speak Cherokee. Since he was white, Thomas avoided the 1838 removal of the Cherokee. A decade later, he purchased property on behalf of local Cherokee who had escaped. Thomas was serving in the North Carolina General Assembly when the secession crisis erupted.[41]

Palmer established Camp Martin on the banks of the Linville River, near his home. His men were part-time soldiers. When not on duty, they were free to return to their homes, looking after their families and tending their farms. The cavalrymen were expected to provide their own mounts. New men continued to trickle in through the month of January. While the activities of the Mitchell Rangers are largely unknown, they captured a few men in January. Adjutant General James G. Martin ordered Palmer to release his captives, once they had taken the Oath of Allegiance, but to keep their arms for "public service." Thomas also broached the idea of a legion while continuing to raise men for his ranger company. At the same time, he announced his intentions of fortifying the mountain passes separating Jackson from Sevier County.[42]

Although not a native of the area, Colonel John B. Palmer was closely tied to the wartime history of the mountains. *North Carolina Division of Archives and History.*

January and February were fairly quiet in the mountain regions. Leadbetter had soldiers stationed throughout the area in East Tennessee. There were companies of the Third Georgia Battalion at Union (Bluff City), Carter's Depot and Elizabethton and four companies in Greeneville. The Twenty-Ninth North Carolina had companies at Midway, the Lick Creek Bridge, Morristown, Strawberry Plains, Flat Creek, Loudon, Charleston and Chattanooga in Tennessee. The Confederate government created the Department of East Tennessee on February 25, 1862, and named Edmund Kirby Smith as departmental commander. Smith was a West Point graduate who had served in the war with Mexico and battled the Seminoles. At First Manassas, he led a brigade. Smith's appointment was in response to the demands of many, including Landon C. Haynes. He wanted Davis to send an aggressive commander who could "restore tone to the army and re-inspire the public confidence." Smith was in Knoxville by March 8. The creation of the department probably had much to do with conditions in middle Tennessee. Forts Henry and Donelson had fallen in early February, and on the twentieth, Governor Harris announced that he was moving the capital from Nashville to Memphis. On February 23, Lincoln appointed Andrew Johnson military governor of Tennessee. Johnson arrived in Nashville and assumed his duties on March 11.[43]

Smith took stock of his new command and did not like what he saw. He wrote that the people were disloyal and the troops under his command "a disorganized mob without head or discipline." To Jefferson Davis, Smith reported, "The force in East Tennessee in great disorganization....All accounts given me were far short of the truth....Regiments and detachments were everywhere acting independently, and without military restraint of any kind." There were only eight thousand troops in East Tennessee under his command, and half of those were at Cumberland Gap. After a quick tour of his department, Smith reported to the War Department: "I repeat, East Tennessee is an enemy's country. The people are against us, and ready to rise whenever an enemy's column makes its appearance. The very troops raised here cannot always be depended upon. They have gone into service, many of them to escape suspicion, prepared to give information to the enemy, and ready to pass over to him when an opportunity offers."[44]

The dissatisfaction was spreading over into Western North Carolina. In March came the first public complaints from the Laurel area of Madison County. In the previous November and December, the Confederate government had placed portions of East Tennessee under martial law. On March 17, a Madison County citizen complained that martial law had driven Tories into the Laurel area "in large ganges." These Tories were "committing all manner of depredations upon the citizens of that region." The writer mentioned murders, robberies and general menacing of citizens but gave no particulars. A letter written ten days later provided

Andrew Johnson lived in Greeneville prior to the war. He was a U.S. senator, military governor of Tennessee, Lincoln's second vice president and president of the United States. *Library of Congress.*

details about new raids. Men from the Laurel community supposedly had raided into Greene County, robbing "several houses, taking all the money they could find and also some powder, telling some of the good citizens at the same time, that the next time they come back, that they intended to burn their houses."[45]

Smith had no troops to send into the countryside. There was a feint toward Cumberland Gap on March 14. Confederate soldiers were rushed from Knoxville to Jacksboro. Then came intelligence that a large number of Federal troops were advancing east, from middle Tennessee. Smith shifted what meager troops he could spare west toward Kingston and Chattanooga, while asking the governors of Alabama and Georgia to send any troops that were armed.

Two events in April changed the nature of the war for those living along the North Carolina–Tennessee border. On April 8, Jefferson Davis suspended civil jurisdiction and the writ of habeas corpus throughout East Tennessee. Criminal courts continued to function, but Smith was granted supervision and had the power to establish military commissions to try criminal cases if civil courts failed to administer justice fairly. Smith also had the power to restrict travel, prohibit the production and sale of alcohol and establish a military police force. Provost marshal Colonel William Churchwell used this power to expel families of well-known Unionists from the area, like the families of Andrew Johnson, Horace Maynard and William G. Brownlow.[46]

More important was the passage of the Confederate Conscription Act. After the surge of voluntary enlistment in 1861, the numbers of men willing to serve in the army had significantly decreased. The loss of territory might have been one reason. Federal forces made inroads on the coast of North Carolina, in Louisiana and Northern Virginia. In Western North Carolina, thousands of men had already volunteered, leaving a dearth of farmers, miller, tanners and other laborers crucial to the survival of a community. For those in East Tennessee, the war was closer to home. The bridge burnings in November 1861 were firsthand information to many. Plus, there were numerous stories of raids throughout the border counties. As early as December 1861, there had been serious talk in the halls of the Confederate Congress of enacting a conscription bill, an attempt to swell the ranks of the Confederate army. The government realized that by the spring of 1862 the Confederate army and any chances of a Southern nation would be crippled when the men in more than 150 regiments, who had enlisted to serve for a single year, were released from service to go home. On March 28, Jefferson Davis submitted a bill to the Congress requiring all white, able-bodied men, between the ages of eighteen and thirty-five, to serve for three years or the war's duration. The bill passed the Confederate Congress on April 16. It was the first draft in American history. Five days later, a supplementary act was passed, exempting teachers, ministers, state employees, industrial workers and slave owners. The legislation also stipulated that all twelve-month volunteers were required to reenlist and to serve an additional two years. A few days later, the Confederate legislatures

An artist's rendition of a pro-Union slaveholding family fleeing East Tennessee. *From* Harper's Weekly.

passed additional legislation that exempted some professional workmen, state employees, ministers, teachers and industrial workers.

Word about the Conscription Act quickly filtered back through the mountains. Those serving in the Confederate army were disturbed by the law. "There is good deal of flusteration in the Ridgment at this time," wrote Watauga County's Bennett Smith, serving in the Thirty-Seventh North Carolina Troops, on April 17, 1862, "cosed by the brutish laws they hav past they have forst awl the 12 months boys during the war or two years I think it is a mean trick I fear our leading men is a corupt body of men." In Greene County, L.B. Headerick complained to Governor Harris that men were unwilling to enter the army "if required to leave their wives and children to starve at the mercy of a far more relentless foe than any of Lincoln's thieves can be."[47]

The conscription law stipulated that regiments in the process of forming had until May 17 to organize. That date was later pushed back until July 8 and then August 1. Men could volunteer until those dates and enlist in a company of their own choosing. Those waiting until later were forced to go into whatever regiment needed men. Palmer's command on the banks of the Watauga River was growing. Many prominent men in the area began to write to the adjutant general, requesting permission to raise companies. One of these was Jacob Bowman, a state representative from Mitchell County. Yancey County's Sheriff William W. Proffitt raised a company. In Watauga County, the Reverend Drury Harmon raised another company. Mexican War veteran John C. Keener raised a company from Mitchell and Caldwell Counties. Store clerk John W. Peak raised an additional company in Yancey County. One of Peak's new recruits, John W. Edwards, provided this glimpse of the recruitment process: "A Word was sent out through the settlement for all of conscript age to come in. Capt. Peak came around and said as I had to go in I had better go in his company. We were acquainted and a little [connected]." All of these companies became members of the Fifty-Eighth North Carolina Troops. Joseph McDowell continued to recruit for his battalion in Buncombe County, as did William Holland Thomas for his command to the west. Between April and August 1862, the six North Carolina counties along the North Carolina–Tennessee border raised thirteen new companies for Confederate service.[48]

Similarly, there were companies raised in Eastern Tennessee as well, albeit not as many. James C. Hodges was attempting to raise a company in Washington County. Hodges wrote to John Crawford, who became colonel of the Sixtieth Tennessee Infantry, that he was having trouble raising his company. "Many of them are not exactly satisfied that the Conscription law will be enforced here, and they desire to hold on till they learn definitely that it will be enforced," Hodges observed. William A. Wash, in Cocke County, was also attempting to recruit Union-leaning men to the Confederate cause. "I cant find a union man," Wash wrote. "All converted in heart and in mind. God forgive them; for many of them never can be by their fellowmen."[49]

A problem that Smith had to address was the exodus of dissenters across state lines. Details about the Conscription Act spread quickly. Men by themselves, in small groups and in huge throngs attempted to work their way through the mountains and into Union lines in Kentucky. In late April, Federal general George W. Morgan, stationed above Cumberland Gap at Cumberland Ford, Kentucky, wrote of a group of 1,000 fugitives attempting to cross when they were caught. At least 100 of their number were captured. Carter Stevenson, the Confederate general in command at Cumberland Gap, reportedly moved infantry, supported by artillery, into the area that the fugitives were attempting to use. A month earlier, there were 1,500 East Tennessee men at Camp Garber, near Barbourville, Kentucky, being organized into regiments. At the same time, there were recruiters in East Tennessee secretly seeking men to cross the lines and join one of the Federal regiments being organized. One of these was Greene County resident Sylvanius H. Thompson and his wife, Sarah. After her husband was killed by Confederates in 1864, Sarah became one of the most famous spies and guides in the area. Local Unionists whom she encountered were told that "if they would meete [her] at a surten plase [she] would see they wold goo thue to the union army." Once an armed group gathered, a pilot signaled with a fire, and the fugitives started for Kentucky. Sevier County guide Will A. McTeer was armed with "an old brass-barreled horse pistol that [his] grandfather carried in the war of 1812." He led a group on July 22, 1862, toward Cumberland Gap. In the first three weeks after the Conscription Act became law, Smith estimated that 7,000 East Tennessee Unionists crossed the mountain into Kentucky and Federal lines.[50]

With his limited number of troops being pulled in different directions, there was little Smith could do. He did issue a proclamation on April 18. Many of the citizens who had crossed state lines had committed treason against their state. If they returned and took the Oath of Allegiance, they would not be "molested or punished on account of past acts or words." A second proclamation was issued on April 23, calling attention to the offer of amnesty and explaining that after thirty days, those who did not come in would have their families sent beyond Confederate lines. "The women and children must be taken care of by husbands and fathers either in East Tennessee or in the Lincoln Government." An East Tennessean wrote to Georgia senator Ben Hill, complaining that nine-tenths of the local men were now absent from their farms. "There are within our borders at this time thousands of families without any male members capable of labor. These helpless women and children are to become a charge upon the public, for whatever may be the sins of their fathers or husbands the Southern people cannot deal cruelly with them." Hill forwarded the letter to Jefferson Davis. "[I]f we are to have hostility of the class called in East Tennessee Union men," Davis unsympathetically responded, "it were better that they should be in the ranks of the enemy than living as spies among us and waiting for opportunity to strike."[51]

Federal regiments made up of East Tennessee men continued to grow. After spending several months hiding out near Greeneville, Robert Johnson, Andrew Johnson's son, made his way to Kentucky. Due to Andrew Johnson's appointment as military governor, Robert received permission to raise a regiment. By early March 1862, he had 220 men organized into five companies. By mid-May, he had 400 soldiers in the Fourth East Tennessee Infantry (U.S.), later designated the First Tennessee Cavalry (U.S.). Three other regiments were in the process of organizing, although the process was slow. Many members of the Second Regiment came from Blount, Sevier and Greene Counties. A large portion of the new recruits chose the cavalry over the infantry, as they had already walked hundreds of miles over the Cumberland Mountains into Kentucky. Cavalry was seen as the best option for dealing with the war in East Tennessee. Infantry could be used to hold a position, like Knoxville or Greeneville, and various points along the line of the railroad. However, in order to chase efficiently the Confederate or guerrilla bands that terrorized seemingly countless communities, a mobile strike force was necessary.[52]

A handful of men slipped across the North Carolina line to join the Federal army in 1862. Shepherd Dugger was just a child during the war, but he later recalled, "One evening in August…eight young men gathered in our cabin….With tearful eyes and affected voices they bade us good-bye and stepped out into the darkness." Even though their family was one of the largest slaveholders in Watauga County, several members of the Banner family chose to cross over the mountain and were a part of that group. Oliver, Columbus, Newton and Henry Banner all joined the Fourth Tennessee Cavalry (U.S.) on August 8, 1862, at Cumberland Gap. Newton supposedly told the officer in charge that "he wanted to fight and if he did not take him in this army, he would join the other side." Newton then took the oath on the corner of three states: Kentucky, Tennessee and Virginia.[53]

William H. Younce, from Ashe County, decided to cross over to the Federals as well. With four others, he set out in August for Kentucky. However, after a couple weeks of "scouting and maneuvering," the group found their route blocked and returned home. In October, Younce and four companions started again for the Federal lines. After crossing over into Tennessee, Younce, despite objections from the others, stopped to visit a family whose beautiful daughter he hoped to woo. She was decidedly pro-Confederate and soon discerned that Younce was trying to avoid conscription. Not long after retiring for the evening, Younce heard the sound of horses. Realizing that he was trapped, Younce dressed, came downstairs and surrendered. It is unclear if the local militia or regular Confederate soldiers were alerted to his presence. Younce was escorted back to Ashe County, and when presented with the choice to either take the oath and voluntarily enlist into a local company or to be conscripted and sent to a different regiment, he took the oath. Soon thereafter, Younce left with fifty others for Tennessee and was mustered into the Fifty-Eighth North Carolina.[54]

Federal forces continued to threaten several key sites, like Cumberland Gap and Chattanooga. Smith was unable to mount any offensive actions. He always feared that if he concentrated his efforts at one point, the Federals would slip in and take Knoxville or Chattanooga. In mid-June, the Federals moved toward Chattanooga, and once again, Smith concentrated his meager forces near Morristown and Rutledge, able to move quickly via railroad to Chattanooga or toward Powell Valley. This time, even the Confederate forces at Cumberland Gap were evacuated. Federal forces took possession of the gap on June 18 and held it until October.

While Smith was concerned about Federal invasions to his north and west, chaos was slowly overtaking the border areas to the south. Many of the problems seemed to stem from the Laurel community of Madison County. In early April, the "men on Laurel commenced their outrages" on the area. A man by the name of Davis was "brutally murdered for refusing to give up

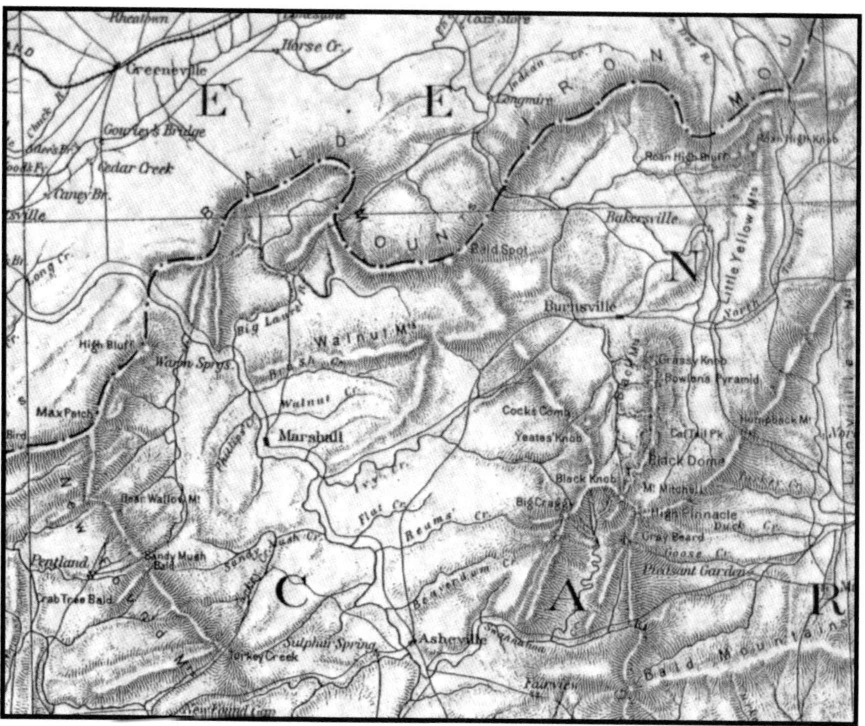

The Laurel area, seen as Big Laurel River on this 1860s map, was a secluded location that provided some degree of refuge to dissidents in the region. *Author's collection.*

his guns" while his family was present. Other local citizens were robbed of "guns, bacon, meal, clothes, and everything they could lay their hands on." The dissidents then captured two recruits from Coleman's battalion, robbed them and then shaved their heads before turning them loose. The newspaper reported that the Madison, Buncombe and Burke County militia companies were called out and, with several companies in the process of organizing for Confederate service, headed toward the Laurel area, capturing many.[55]

That same month, it was reported that Confederate troops from Knoxville were sent into the Laurel area to sweep out the dissidents. The troops were under the command of Colonel James W. Gillespie and the Fifth East Tennessee Infantry, later known as the Forty-Third Tennessee Infantry. The *Asheville News* reported on the movements:

> *They found the tories scattered through the mountains, in laurel thickets and in the mountain gorges, where it was impossible to reach them with the small force in pursuit.... They commenced bush-whacking our troops from the time they struck the head of Laurel Creek, and kept it up until they got out of the mountains. They killed one soldier by the name of Morgan in Capt. Goodman's company, and wounded two others, one seriously but we hope not fatally.—What amount of destruction was done to the marauders by our troops is not known, but from the way some of them tumbled over and kick when our men fired upon them, would suppose they killed some fifteen or twenty. They are certain they killed some two or three of the Sheltons, who are ring leaders of this marauding party. This is only giving them a foretaste of what will follow, as our authorities are determined to break up this nest of thieving tories and robbers. Lieut. Tonkin of Capt. Goodman's company had a small buck shot strike him near the groin, but hitting his pocket book prevented the ball from entering his flesh. The ball passed through nine folds of leather, and several papers and bank bills, lodging against the back of the pocket book, dropping into one of the pockets of the book.*[56]

The editor of the *Asheville News* was censured by newspapers in Raleigh. They contended that the accounts of events in Madison County were "more imaginary than real." "To say that the late difficulties in Madison were 'more imaginary than real,' is to write down the authorities of the counties of Madison and Buncombe, with General Erwin as their head, a set of asses," the *Asheville News* fired back. "Our statements were based upon facts on which official action was taken, and were substantially true in all respects. Pity the Confederate soldiers killed by the outlaws on Laurel cannot be aroused from their gory beds, and made to believe that their 'taking off' was 'more imaginary than real'! Pity that poor Davis, a good Southern man, shot down in the midst of his family for refusing to surrender his gun, cannot be brought back to life, with the assurance that his base assassination was 'more imaginary than real'!"[57]

There were not many reports of trouble in the Toe River Valley or east into Watauga or Ashe County that spring, summer and fall. To the west, however, was a different story. On June 14, a group of eighteen, deputized by the local Jackson County sheriff, went to the home of Uriah Burns to arrest Burns, along with his wife, daughter and son for assault and battery on Adeline Burns, Uriah's daughter-in-law. The man in charge of the arresting party was Sam Burchfield, Uriah's brother-in-law. The son was arrested, but the other three charged the arresting party. Uriah was armed with a rifle and the mother and daughter with an axe and knife. As Uriah started to cross a fence, he was shot and killed. Later, several of the arresting party were arrested and hauled off to superior court in Buncombe and tried. William B. Garrett, J.M. Morris and R.L.D. Burchfield were found guilty and sentenced to be hanged in January 1863. Six others were found guilty of manslaughter and sentenced to six months in prison, a charge the judge would remit if they voluntarily joined the Confederate army. When the story first broke, the eighteen were described as Tories, and Burns was reportedly killed because his six sons were Confederate soldiers and he himself "was also a volunteer." It is possible that the death of Uriah actually had nothing to do with the war and was simply some feud between families, but the media took the opportunity to depict it as politically motivated violence.[58]

At the same time as the Buncombe County trial for the group charged with killing Burns, another man was on trial as well. As the local story goes, Haywood County sheriff John P. Noland was following JoAnn Robinson. She had been to visit her husband, being held for desertion, in the county jail. Noland believed that Robinson could lead him to others. Near the crest of a ridge, she began to sing the hymn "How Firm a Foundation," a prearranged signal. Suddenly, a shot rang out, and Noland fell from his horse, wounded in the throat. He died there in a gap on the ridge that now bears his name. James H. Franklin was arrested for the murder of Noland, tried and then sentenced to hang on January 16, 1863. Before the sentence could be carried out, a group of men, ranging between twenty-five and forty, stormed into Waynesville on the night of November 19. The jailer had his life threatened, and the "tories cursed and insulted several ladies, made threats of burning the town if interfered with, and committed numerous outrages."[59]

Zebulon Baird Vance, from Buncombe County, served as colonel of the Twenty-Sixth North Carolina Troops and then as wartime governor of the state of North Carolina. *North Carolina Museum of History.*

Locals complained that there was a huge camp of dissidents, deserters and Unionists entrenched on the Haywood-Cocke County line. One account placed the number at "several hundred," while another account estimated just over one thousand. Couriers were sent to Knoxville, begging for soldiers to be sent to the area. John B. Fitzgerald, a Haywood County lawyer, took the opportunity to write to the recently sworn-in governor, Zebulon Baird Vance, about local conditions. The "deserters, Tories, and rascals" hid out in the mountainous area between Waynesville and the Tennessee line. When the militia or local troops closed in, the dissidents simply crossed state lines, moving beyond the jurisdiction of the pursuing state forces. "Perhaps no section affords such advantages for concealment and evading law as this, and if not broken up, and it's found, such as get in there with impunity, it gives encouragement to deserters from the army, tories and outlaws in the surrounding country, and such puts in jeopardy the homes, property and even lives of our citizens, for these scoundrels must live," Fitzgerald believed.[60]

It seemed that the scattered Confederate forces were doing all they could on the Tennessee side during the summer and fall of 1862. While one Confederate company was moving down the Newport Road in Sevier County, it was ambushed, and one man was wounded in the arm. The column continued on, coming to the home of Unionist Mark Byrd, whom they shot; then they burned his house. Later on, they came upon the home of another Unionist, Mark Fox, whom they cursed for being a Tory. When Fox cursed back, they killed him. In Cocke County, Halcomb Lowell was captured by local Confederate conscription officer James Harley. Lowell escaped from the locked cabin where he was confined and, four months later, ambushed Harley and his son, killing both of them. In Greene County, between eighty and one hundred dissidents fortified a still house belonging to a man named Wattenbarder and spread out into the surrounding area. After robbing a Mr. Powell in Hawkins County, they "put…eight or ten balls through his head."[61]

Smith issued a new appeal to the Unionists in East Tennessee on August 13, imploring them to come back to Tennessee and take the oath of allegiance. They would be given cash for any weapons they brought. The following day, Smith moved most of his command toward Kentucky, bypassing the isolated Federals entrenched at Cumberland Gap. John P. McCowan was left in charge of East Tennessee as the bulk of Confederate forces moved toward central Kentucky. McCowan was left with three infantry regiments and an undisclosed amount of cavalry to protect the railroad and keep the dissidents at bay. John Palmer's new regiment, the Fifty-Eighth North Carolina Troops, moved from the banks of the Linville River to Haynesville (Johnson City) in July. By mid-August, one company was at Carter's Depot and two others at Zollicoffer. The Fifty-Ninth Tennessee, organized in June 1862, had three companies stationed in Knoxville, four at Strawberry Plains, one in Morristown, one at Holston and one at Flat Creek. The Sixty-Second North Carolina Troops was in the process of organizing at Jonesborough, while the Sixty-Third Tennessee Infantry was organizing in Knoxville. The Sixtieth North Carolina Troops was still back at Warm Springs in North Carolina. The last three regiments were most likely unarmed at this time, except for what weapons could be brought from home.[62]

Even with the majority of Confederate forces gone, there were still efforts to curb the disloyalty in the area. The newspaper in Jonesborough reported that six men were arrested in one week, charged "with starting for Kentucky." In late September, a portion of what became the Sixty-Fourth North Carolina Troops swept through Sevier County. Unionists were supposedly gathered at Wear's Cave. At the approach of the Confederates, these men scattered, and the Confederate cavalry spread out to scour the mountainsides. The newspaper reported that fifty were captured. Along the banks of the Watauga River, in Johnson County, several Southerners were attacked by Thomas Frits. As the party walked down a path, Frits "rushed from the undergrowth with Bowie knife in hand upon a loyal Southern man…stabbing him twenty-three times." The others were forced to take to their heels and hide in the woods. "This county is a perfect den of thieves and tories," Corporal John Moreland, who witnessed the deed, complained.[63]

Ashe County's William H. Younce regretted his decision to take the oath and join the Confederate army. After two weeks in the camp of the Fifty-Eighth North Carolina, he and three others "flanked the guards" and deserted. During the day, they kept to the woods, while at night, they allowed themselves to use roads. Traveling through the mountains fatigued the men, and the provisions they had smuggled out of camp soon ran low. Spying a farmhouse one evening, they went and asked for food, professing to be Confederates soldiers on their way home on leave. They spent the night but discovered the next morning that their host was the local Confederate enrolling officer. Overnight, he had sent for troops and arrested Younce and his companions the next morning. As they were ushered out on the porch to prepare for breakfast, two of Younce's companions bolted for the woods. They had cleared a fence and were twenty-five yards from the cabin when four of the guards opened fire. While all the shots missed, the two stopped, returned and, after finishing breakfast, were started back to the jail in Rogersville and the Fifty-Eighth North Carolina.[64]

Robert A. Ragan (Reagan), who was working on a farm in Cocke County, also sought to escape north. He was teaching school in 1862 when he was arrested and sent to Knoxville. Ragan used his connections to Confederate postmaster John H. Reagan to gain his release but was forced into hiding when he returned home. Learning that a group was leaving from Greene County for Kentucky, Ragan joined in, only to drop out after a "strong premonition of danger." Later it was learned that the group had been intercepted. Ragan camped out near family members, often changing locations between Cocke and Greene Counties and sometimes wearing women's clothes. When learning that another group was heading out, he went to his father-in-law's home to wait. Confederate soldiers noticed his presence, and Ragan just barely escaped out a back door, injuring his foot as he jumped over a fence. Unable to keep up, he returned to hiding. Finally, in July 1863, he learned of yet another group numbering about one hundred men heading out, this one led by George W. Kirk. They made it safely to Camp Dick Robinson, Kentucky, where Ragan enlisted. He soon responded to the call to guide others to Union lines and returned to Greene County.[65]

There were men who took up the occupation of professional guides. One of the most legendary was Carter County's Daniel Ellis. Even though much of his story cannot be substantiated, shortly after the war, Ellis left a detailed account of his exploits guiding men to the Federal lines. Ellis played a minor role in the bridge burnings before being chased back into the mountains. In early August 1862, he made his first trip to Kentucky, partially by himself and at times with a more experienced guide. On his return to Carter County, local people, along with refugees from North Carolina, implored Ellis to guide them to Union lines. At the end of August, he started with a group of seventy-five from Valley Forge, bound for Cumberland Gap. They moved into Sullivan County, crossing the Holston River below Pactolus Ferry in a stolen boat, and then camped at White Oak Flats, "a very noted hiding place for the fugitives from rebel oppression." On the return trip, Ellis procured the use of another guide, and he set out for Carter County. He was spotted by Confederate soldiers in Washington County. As they pursued him, he ducked off the road and hid under a "chincapin bush" until they passed. Ellis then hid in a cornfield until night. Thinking he was in the clear, Ellis continued, only to meet the same cavalry in the road. This time, he stepped behind a tree, evading capture and returning home without further incident. Ellis made two additional trips before the year ended.[66]

As 1862 came to a close, there was serious trouble brewing throughout the mountain counties. Conscription had driven many across the state boundaries and into the Federal army in Kentucky. Others had chosen to

Many men used guides, such as Daniel Ellis, to guide them through the mountains to the Federal lines. *From* The Thrilling Adventures of Daniel Ellis.

remain behind, hiding in the remote sections of the mountains, dependent on their families or ingenuity to survive. The war in the Laurel community of Madison County was spilling over into Tennessee. It was a war within a war to which neither side seemed willing to commit the resources to win. The same is true for the war in the mountain region as a whole, but especially in East Tennessee. Middle Tennessee and Western Tennessee fell to Federal forces in early 1862. Yet pro-Union East Tennessee was still held by Confederate forces as the year ended. The internal conflict in the mountains would only get worse.

3

1863

"There Is No Doubt a Considerable Amount of Renegades Scattered Over the Mountains"

On December 15, 1862, J.A. Reeves wrote to Governor Vance about the lack of salt in his native Ashe County. According to Reeves, there was a large surplus of hogs, but local residents could not procure enough salt to supply their needs. Pork was a major staple in the diets of rural people, and they required salt to preserve it and other foodstuffs. Without salt to preserve their perishable food supply, and with a short growing season, the people faced a real threat to their survival. As the war entered its second year, the loss of men working in local industries was having a profound influence on mountain society. Along with millers and other workers, salt makers became less common as they were taken away by the war. In addition, the conflict made travel and transport of salt more difficult, if not impossible. Some local citizens had come to the conclusion that the only way to address the problem was to march to Saltville, Virginia, and take needed salt by force. "I can get 3 to 4 hundred men in one days notice to start," Reeves wrote to Vance, conveying the locals' intent to take matters into their own hands.[67]

The North Carolina General Assembly had recognized the problem of the salt supply in early 1862 and created the position of salt agent for each county. These counties' court systems then appointed subagents for each district within the county. It was the duty of the county agent, once he had acquired salt, to allocate it to the subagents, who then distributed it to the people at cost. For those living in the eastern and central portions of the state, salt could be obtained from the state salt works along the coast. People living in the mountain counties, however, were dependent on the salt coming from Saltville. Buncombe County lawyer and politician Nicholas Woodfin was appointed as the salt agent for North Carolina at Saltville. He erected his own furnace and kettles and employed slaves to help turn the saline water into granular salt. The county salt commissioner, or his appointee, was responsible for transporting the final product. Cornelia Henry recorded in her diary in November 1862 that George Peak was heading to Saltville with five wagons, presumably to collect salt for distribution in Buncombe County. Being salt agent was a difficult job. It was reported in Yancey County that the county salt agent quit three times in one year. Salt was distributed only to the pro-Confederate families. Those with Unionist leanings, or those who had family members avoiding conscription, were supposedly excluded. Without salt, a family could not survive.[68]

All throughout Western North Carolina were little pockets or conclaves of Confederate resistance. Some of the individuals in these areas were truly loyal to the Union. Others were simply dissident by nature, not caring for either side, and at times used the war as an excuse to perpetuate long-standing feuds. One such area of unrest was the Shelton Laurel community of Madison County. In many ways, this community represents the war in the mountains at its worst, and the shocking violence there is usually the sole account of the local war that is known to those outside the region. Founded in the late 1700s by two brothers, David and Martin Shelton, the community is located just over four miles from the Tennessee line and ten miles from the county seat in Marshall. Eventually, the Sheltons were joined by three or four other families. These families chose the location primarily for the isolation it provided.

That isolation did insulate the residents from the troubles of the 1860s. It was rumored that the Laurel Creek area was a haven for those attempting to evade the fallout from the bridge-burning incidents. As early as March 1862, there were reports of up to one thousand Tories in the area, "committing all manner of depredations." Captain David Fry, one of the leaders of the bridge burners, was rumored to be in the vicinity. At least once in 1862, regular Confederate troops from East Tennessee, along with the militia from surrounding North Carolina counties, had moved through the area in an attempt to clear out the dissidents. One story recounted in 1863 was that the man guiding the Confederate and militia forces into the Laurel community was killed. The drought that hit the mountain area in the summer and fall of 1862, coupled with the severity of the winter, undoubtedly made some families desperate. At the same time, it was reported that there were Federal officers and recruiters in the area, stirring up strife.[69]

Exact numbers of dissidents on Laurel Creek at the turn of the year are difficult to pinpoint. One writer estimated the group to be around 80. Another puts their number at 150, largely Confederate deserters who had returned home with their equipment. There were complaints that the group had crossed the state line, raiding homes in the Flag Pond area of present-day Unicoi County, "taking money, guns, clothes, meat, and every thing they could carry away, making women and children strip off their shoes, socks and clothes for them, and left many families almost destitute of clothing, bedding or provisions." Committing these outrages were men of all ages, some as young as ten, according to one correspondent. The youngest "were the most active rogues" in the group.[70]

Next, the marauders turned their attention on the town of Marshall. Late in the evening on January 8, 1863, the miscreants moved on the county seat. They were rumored to have taken salt stockpiled for pro-Confederate families. After ransacking the courthouse and destroying county records, they broke into a local boardinghouse belonging to A.E. Baird and "robbed it of all the blankets and other bed furniture." From there, they entered the home of Colonel Allen. Many of the robbers were reported to be deserters from Allen's command. From Mrs. Allen, they demanded her keys for various trunks and bureaus, threatening her with death if she did not comply. Axes were used when the keys were not surrendered. The furniture was carried away or smashed, and the bandits also made off with all of the clothes, shoes and even the blankets from the beds where Allen's sick children lay. One contemporary account stated that Mrs. Allen was forced to strip off all of her clothing, leaving her exposed and humiliated. As the group, reported to be mostly made up of young men from the Laurel area, returned, they robbed the Farnsworth house, emptying the bed ticks and filling them with clothes and other stolen plunder. One account claimed that as they made their way through the mountains, they "ravaged the whole country." Several went out in search of the party, including Captain John Peak, Sixty-Fourth North Carolina Troops. Peak was at home on leave and struck in the arm by a volley fired by the looters. His wound forced him out of the army a year later.[71]

The militia from the surrounding counties began to assemble in Asheville on January 13. Orders came from the adjutant general in Raleigh: Colonel John W. McElroy was instructed to assume command of the militias from Yancey, Madison and Buncombe Counties in order to put "down this armed

Lawrence Allen's house still stands in the town of Marshall. *Author's collection.*

resistance," arresting "all deserters and conscripts ages 18–35." The raiders had threatened Asheville and the armory. Portions of the militia swept through neighboring Madison and Yancey Counties. William Henry, who attached himself to the staff of Marcus Erwin, wrote home that the militia had "killed some 30 tories & taken 16 prisoners."[72]

Word filtered back to Knoxville of the raid in Marshall. Major General Henry Heth was now in charge of the Department of East Tennessee. He wrote to Governor Vance on January 17 of the force he was sending to contend with the crisis. Brigadier General William G.M. Davis exercised overall command of the expedition. Davis established his headquarters at Warm Springs. Major William M. Garrett was selected to lead part of the force. For the mission, Garrett commanded two hundred members of his own Sixty-Fourth North Carolina Troops, a company of cavalry under Captain Thomas N. Nelson and thirty Indians from Thomas's Legion. Heth then sent Colonel William Thomas with two hundred Cherokee Indians into the area as well. Major Nelson began working his way toward the Laurel area, while Thomas scoured other portions of Madison before moving toward Haywood, Jackson and Cherokee Counties, ending up in Clay County, Georgia. At the same time, Colonel George Folk worked in conjunction with the forces in Madison, taking a portion of his cavalry through Washington, Carter and Johnson Counties.[73]

A segment of Folk's command was in East Tennessee as early as September 1862. By the first of January, a member of Folk's regiment, the Seventh Battalion, North Carolina Cavalry, reported being in camp at Mount Taylor in Carter County. The regiment's orders were to capture or disperse "a body of disloyal men" from North Carolina who were said to be organizing themselves into a group to "resist" the authorities of the Confederate States and were also joining the enemy in Kentucky. Chief on the most wanted list was a James Taylor, reportedly a captain in the Second East Tennessee Cavalry. William Penland, a member of Folk's command, wrote that Taylor had a group of seventy men and had "been capturing soldiers, stealing and plundering from the citizens of…Carter and Johnson" for some time. In mid-January, Taylor's band burned the home of Mrs. Carter, near Elizabethton, taking a considerable amount of corn and forage. Around January 23, Folk, along with forty of his men, were out patrolling along the Watauga River near Fish Spring, when they spied members of Taylor's band on the other side of the river. Folk ordered his detachment to ford the Watauga, and when Taylor's men saw them, they abandoned their camp and moved up the mountain, taking up a position on a bluff. As Folk moved in, Taylor's men opened fire. Thomas Newman, a private under Folk, was struck and killed, and it is possible that another private, David Wagner, was also killed in the skirmish. Several others reported having their clothes shot full of holes. Folk ordered his troopers to dismount, and Taylor's men fled. Taylor was shot and killed, as was Samuel Tatum. Three others were captured. George Kite and Alexander Dugger were hanged on the spot. Because he was just a boy, the other prisoner was sent to Knoxville.[74]

George N. Folk led a small band of men on a raid on a dissident camp at Fish Springs in early 1863. *North Carolina Division of Archives and History.*

There are, of course, differing viewpoints on the skirmish at Fish Springs. Daniel Ellis lived in the area but did not witness the events. Writing after the war, he stated that Taylor's band was armed with only an old pistol and a knife. According to Ellis, these arms "so enraged the rebel demons that they rushed forward like blood-thirsty tigers, and butchered these poor men in cold blood, without pity and without mercy." James Taylor had tried to surrender, Ellis claimed, but "these incarnate devils ran up" and shot "the top of his head off with a musket. Two of them then caught him by his feet, and pitched him violently over a large rock down a steep declivity, which bruised his body and broke his limbs in a most shocking manner." Large rocks were then hurled on Taylor's lifeless form, and then he was robbed of a watch and money, Ellis wrote. Ellis then asserted that Tatum was killed in likewise manner, but surprisingly, Tatum actually survived the war. The three others ran but eventually surrendered, "imploring for mercy," claiming that the only crime they were guilty of was "trying to keep out of the Southern army." These three had their hands tied behind them and were then "taken to a bending sapling and hung....[T]hey were hung so as not to break their necks, but rather to be choked to death by degrees." A member of Folk's party, Captain Roby Brown of the Johnson County Home Guard, "had a complete frolic around them while they were struggling in all the agonies of a terrible death." According to Ellis, Brown would strike them with his gun and then "dance up to them, and turn them around violently, telling them to 'face their partner'...while they, with tongues as black as ink protruding out of their mouths, and eyes bursting from their sockets, exhibited a spectacle of horror which was enough to strike terror to the very soul of any person." Local Unionists later buried the victims, Ellis wrote.[75]

Moving his command of Cherokees from Greeneville toward the mountains, William H. Thomas wrote to his wife: "There is no doubt a considerable amount of renegades scattered over the mountains." Thomas's command spread out, covering much more territory than what was included in his original assignment. One company was positioned in the Iron Mountains, possibly in conjunction with Folk's men. A group of Thomas's men working in the Cades Cove area of the Smoky Mountains reported that they had "[c]aptured and took one hundred and thirty-four prisoners and killed twenty bush whackers & wounded several others." More movements made by Thomas's men are largely missing from the historical record.[76]

Confederate cavalry under Captain Nelson swept into the Laurel Valley. General Davis reported on January 20 that Nelson had killed twelve men and captured twenty others. Writing to Governor Vance, Davis believed that there was "no treasonable organization of citizens in North Carolina" and that the raiders in Marshall "were instigated by desire of plunder." Davis praised McElroy and the militia, stating that they were "active and zealous in searching for outlaws." Davis told McElroy the militia could go home and attend to "domestic affairs" but did turn over those captured to the militia to stand trial in Madison County.[77]

Captain Roby Brown of the Johnson County Home Guard, dancing before the bodies of dissidents. *From* The Thrilling Adventures of Daniel Ellis.

However, word soon began to circulate that the Laurel War was not quite over. The events that occurred over the next couple of weeks are clouded in controversy. According to the often-repeated story, the commander of the Sixty-Fourth North Carolina gained permission from Henry Heth to return to Madison County with a portion of the regiment in order to sort out the problems. Snow was falling as they entered Laurel Valley from two different directions. Eight armed robbers were killed before the group rendezvoused at Bill Shelton's home. A skirmish at the Shelton place killed six more dissidents. On the night of January 26, Colonel Allen received word that his six-year-old son had died and his four-year-old daughter was extremely ill. Allen rode out of Laurel Valley with an escort of four men. Several shots were fired at them and his horse struck. However, Allen arrived home in time for his daughter to die in his arms. After burying his child, Allen returned to his regiment and the Laurel Valley, probably on January 28. Six more dissidents were killed that day. Allen returned to Knoxville, while James Keith took charge of the men. His men fanned out into the surrounding mountains and hollers. Women were rounded up, whipped, tortured, hanged and then cut down, all in an effort to entice them to disclose the locations of those in hiding. Immediately after the war, one writer complained that the Confederates burned numerous dwellings and assaulted a young married woman, who in 1865 was a "maniac." Eventually, Keith captured fifteen prisoners who were told that they would be taken to Knoxville and tried for their alleged misdeeds. After being detained in Laurel for the weekend, thirteen prisoners were taken north. The other two had escaped. A few miles down the road, the group halted, and the prisoners were escorted into a grotto, or cleared area. Five of the prisoners were ordered to kneel, and a squad of soldiers stopped ten paces in front of them. "For God's sake, men, you are not going to shoot us? If you are going to murder us at least give us time to pray," one of the prisoners reportedly exclaimed. The request was denied. Some of the soldiers seemed to hesitate, and they were instructed, "Fire or you will take their place." Ten muskets cracked the silence of that snowy morning, and four of the prisoners fell over dead. The fifth was gut shot and was shot again, this time in the head. Five additional prisoners were ushered forward. Thirteen-year-old David Shelton pleaded with the soldiers, "You have killed my father and brothers. You have shot my father in the face; do not shoot me in the face." Once again the rifles rang out, and four fell dead. "You have killed my old father and my three brothers; you have shot me in both arms—I forgive you all this—I can get well. Let me go home to my mother and sisters," David pleaded. He was dragged back into line and shot dead. Likewise, the other three met the same fate. A shallow grave was dug, and the thirteen bloodied corpses were thrown in and covered. A Virginian attached to the Sixty-Fourth supposedly jumped upon the pile of bodies and sang, "Pat Juda for me, while I dance the damned scoundrels down to and through hell."[78]

For decades, people have debated the validity of portions of the story behind the Shelton Laurel Massacre. Henry Heth supposedly authorized Lieutenant Colonel James Keith, a resident of the area, to return to Madison County, taking a portion of the Sixty-Fourth North Carolina. "I want no reports from you about your course at Laurel. I do not want to be troubled with any prisoners and the last one of them should be killed," Keith later claimed were his verbal orders from Heth. The Sixty-Fourth was stationed at Jacksboro, at least on paper. In reality, the men of the regiment were spread out. Companies C, F, G and K were believed to be positioned at Jacksboro; Companies A, H and I were at Big Creek Gap. Companies B, D and E were assigned to return to North Carolina. Of the returning three companies, only Company D actually had originated in Madison County. The others were from Henderson and Polk Counties. Colonel Allen's postwar account, chronicled by then-lieutenant Josiah P. Gaston, whose company was not sent back, places Allen in Madison County right before the massacre took place. Yet Allen was in Knoxville on January 30, preparing to stand trial for lying about the whereabouts of his adjutant, who was away in Virginia on an unauthorized assignment. Gaston's account locates Allen back in North Carolina between January 25 and February 1, 1863. The Shelton Laurel widows, in a petition to Congress after the war, date the massacre to January 18. The letter from Davis to Vance gives a date of January 20. Then there is the problem of the number of people actually killed. Davis writes that his men had killed twelve. According to the description provided by Gaston, if all the dissidents dispatched over several days actually died, the number of killed is above thirty.[79]

Back in Raleigh, Vance was baffled by the complicated and confusing events as he tried to make sense of what was actually transpiring in the troubled Laurel community. He had implored Secretary of War Seddon on January 20 "to send every available man to" address the salt raid. A telegraphed message from Heth to Vance on January 21 informed the governor that Captain Nelson's cavalry had killed thirteen and captured twenty. "I hope you will not relax until the tories are crushed," Vance telegraphed back. Yet at the same time, he cautioned Heth, "But do not let our excited people deal too harshly with these misguided men. Please have the captured delivered to the proper authorities for trial." On January 31, word filtered back to Vance that some of the prisoners had been shot without a hearing or trial, despite his admonitions to the contrary. Two days later, Vance learned that Allen, Keith and a portion of the Sixty-Fourth North Carolina were involved in the incident. On February 9, Vance asked Augustus Merrimon, solicitor for the Eighth District, to both prosecute the surviving prisoners taken from the Laurel community and investigate the execution of the other prisoners.[80]

Merrimon had a difficult time finding answers in the tangled and distorted accounts of what happened in January in Madison County. He confessed in a letter on February 16 that all of his information came from "a most reliable source" but that personally "he had no knowledge of my own touching the shooting of several prisoners in Laurel." He had heard reports that at least thirteen had been killed. "[S]ome of them were not taken in arms but at their homes....[A]ll...were prisoners at the time they were shot....[A]ll this was done by order of Lieut. Col. James A. Keith....I suggest they [the men from the Sixty-Fourth] are all guilty of murder." Merrimon again wrote Vance on February 24, confirming much of what he had previously written. Of the thirteen killed, eight were "probably" not involved in the raid on Marshall. "I suppose they were shot on suspicion," Merrimon wrote, but he also confessed that he could not "learn the names of the soldiers who shot them." This time, Merrimon had a list of names to go with the bodies buried in the shallow grave outside the Laurel community: "Elison King (desperate man); Jo Woods (desperate man); Will Shelton...Aronnata Shelton, fourteen years old (was not at Marshall); James Shelton (Old Jim)...James Shelton, Jr., seventeen years old...David Shelton, thirteen years old (was not in the raid); James Madcap...Rob Shelton (Stob Rod); David Shelton (brother of Stob Rod); Joseph Cleandon, fifteen or sixteen years old; Halen Moore...Wade Moore." What Merrimon did not mention, and might not have known, was that at least five members of the group—Will Shelton, David Shelton, Halen and Henry Moore and Elison King—were all Confederate deserters. There is also a possibility that some of the younger prisoners were actually part of the violent gang of ten- to fifteen-year-olds whom local citizens complained were routinely raiding nearby homes. Vance wanted Keith to stand trial for the murder of the thirteen prisoners, regardless of the crimes they might have committed themselves. For months, Vance wrote to Secretary of War Seddon, urging action on the matter. Keith and Allen were both allowed to resign, however, and managed to slip through the cracks of justice.[81]

After the war, rumors surfaced that one or more of the Kirk brothers from Greene County, Tennessee, actually led the Laurel men on the Marshall salt

George W. Kirk (*right*), pictured with his father, Alexander Kirk (*standing*), and brother John Kirk (*left*), was promoted to colonel of the Third North Carolina Mounted Infantry (U.S.) and led this band of "scoundrels and thieves" throughout the mountains of Western North Carolina and East Tennessee. *Courtesy of Matt Bumgarner.*

raid. A Jonesborough newspaper reported in October 1865 that "a brave fellow named Kirk" led the Laurel citizens on the raid in Marshall. The *New York Herald* reported in December 1868 that a "Captain Kirk," a former tailor in East Tennessee, gave the command to move toward the town. There was a James Kirk, an apprentice shoemaker in the 1860 census, who would become a captain in the Eighth Tennessee Cavalry in late 1863. Many thought the leader of the band of raiders was James's older brother, George W. Kirk, a house carpenter living in Greene County prior to the war. The editor of the *Greensboro Patriot* in 1870 titled the event "Kirk's Salt Raid." It is possible that both Kirks were involved.[82]

It is difficult to pinpoint the activities of George W. Kirk during the first years of the war. Kirk was born on July 26, 1837, in Greene County, the son of Alexander Kirk. It is rumored that he originally enlisted in the Confederate army, but that information is unsubstantiated. His location prior to August 1862 is unclear. The *Greensboro Patriot* reported, "During the first year of the war, Kirk skulked in the woods, not identifying himself with either side of the belligerents. On account of his frequent raids on the defenceless women and children of the mountain districts of his State—Tennessee—[he] was forced to seek shelter in the Laurel mountains of Madison county in North Carolina." Kirk was described as being six feet tall, with a dark complexion, hair and eyes. He originally enlisted at Cumberland Gap on July 1, 1862, and was mustered into the First Tennessee Cavalry (U.S.) on August 31, 1862, at the rank of private. He transferred to the Fourth Tennessee Infantry (U.S.) on January 14, 1863, although he does not appear on the records until June of that year. On June 30, he transferred to the Eighth Tennessee Cavalry (U.S.). Yet the records of the Eighth Cavalry have him appointed as a captain, commanding Company D, on April 22, 1863. He went on to be a part of at least one other Federal regiment before the end of the war.[83]

Some might have believed that the Confederate sweep through the mountains of Western North Carolina and East Tennessee would quell the dissidents. Yet as winter slipped into spring, small uprisings continued to break the tranquility of the region. Daniel Ellis recalled that after the Sixty-Fourth North Carolina left, another group of Confederate soldiers paid a visit to the Laurel community. Several families were ordered into one house, and the vacant houses were burned, while any livestock found were killed and all provisions taken. One local widow, Lucinda Carter, had fourteen hogs killed and thrown into her house, followed by her "house-dog." According to Ellis, when children tried to beg food from the Confederate soldiers, they were told to do without, "or else you must go to Old Abe for it." Several women were arrested and taken to Greeneville, where they were "detained for several days, subjected to gross abuse and indignity," before being released. About that same time, Stephen Thomas, a secessionist from neighboring Haywood County, complained that the Unionists had crossed from East Tennessee at several different points and were "robbing stealing and plundering almost all the time and shooting at Southern men when ever they can….They have taken nearly all the guns in the neighborhood…. They take bacon clothing thread and even women's clothing." A month later, William Penland, a sergeant in the Seventh Battalion North Carolina Cavalry, stationed in the Greasy Cove section of Washington County, wrote home about encountering bushwhackers nearby. Any place there was a thicket, there was a camp, Penland believed. In one of these thickets, three bushwhackers were found. While attempting to escape, one of the three was shot and killed.[84]

Penland related that his own company was spread out in small detachments in the area. Probably at no time during the war were there so many Confederates roaming the mountains. Dan Ellis complained that Carter County was full of Indians. An entire company of those "red savages" was posted some one hundred yards from his house, awaiting his arrival. Ellis had just returned from piloting yet another group over the mountains. Just a few days earlier, the home of fellow Carter County farmer and local politician Isaac L. Nave had been robbed. "Fiddler John" Smith was caught and accused of being a part of the gang that had robbed the Nave home. He was locked up in the jail in Elizabethton and, after a trial, was taken by soldiers four and a half miles from Elizabethton and executed. One of the shooters then cut off Smith's finger to remove a ring that he was wearing. "They all say that the people of East Tennessee are almost ready to give up," complained Greeneville attorney Robert Crawford in a letter to Andrew Johnson in June. "[R]obbery, theft and murder is of daily occurrence. The men over forty-five years of age of the Secession party have organized themselves into home Guard Companies and are prowling over the County searching the Houses of Union men examining their letters and private papers and taking off such things as they need. The Indians are scattered over Greene & Jefferson Counties, doing the work of Treason, Hell & secession." In Cocke County, local residents complained when members of the Fifth Georgia Battalion appeared in the Parrottsville community, taking horses and robbing Robert S. Roadman of $6,000.[85]

By July 1863, the war had arrived on a personal level in just about every community along the border. In Carter County, Confederate enrollment officer William P. Brooks was ambushed and killed while chasing the Heatherly gang. Heatherly's bunch was also reported in Washington County, raiding homes along the Nolichucky River. The men preferred to strike at night, filling bedsheets and sacks with everything they could find. At the Byrd Bayless farm, the raiders "piled heaps of bed clothing, and combustibles upon a bed, and set fire to them." They left the family inside, "fastening the door on the outside." On Coldspring Mountain, on the Madison-Greene County line, David Shelton Jr., his nephew William Shelton, thirteen-year-old-Millard Haire and several others were scouting in the area. The Sheltons were members of the Second North Carolina Mounted Infantry (U.S.). As the story goes, members of the Sixty-Fourth North Carolina surrounded the cabin where they were staying. As they poured out of the cabin, the Sheltons and Haire were killed, while four others were wounded and captured. The rest escaped and eventually made their way back to their commands. In Yancey County, a local citizen complained to Governor Vance that the home of Melchizedek Chandler was robbed and his wife threatened with hanging. When Chandler returned, he abandoned his home and moved closer to the relative safety of Burnsville. Local militia commander John W. McElroy had to post guards to prevent his own home from being burned. At the end of the month, R.V. Blackstock wrote Vance, describing how Tories

Carter County's Daniel Ellis served as a guide during the war. In the last few months, he joined the Thirteenth Tennessee Cavalry. *From* The Thrilling Adventures of Daniel Ellis.

had burned wagons and a threshing machine, while a Confederate officer from the Twenty-Fifth North Carolina caught a group of deserters from a Virginia regiment, killing one and capturing four; the other nine escaped.[86]

Governor Vance had to take action. Earlier that year, there had been an incident in Yadkin County. A group of dissidents and Confederate deserters, with plans to cross over the mountains and into Federal lines, was held up at the Bond School House. The militia attacked the group, and several were killed, while others were captured or made their escape. When four of the captives were convicted of murder, the state supreme court discharged the men, ruling that according to North Carolina law, Vance and the militia did not have the authority to arrest deserters and conscripts. That power "pertained to the Confederate authorities alone." With no Confederate Supreme Court in play, the ruling of a state supreme court was considered the law of the land. Vance revoked a previous order to his militia commanders regarding arresting violators of Confederate conscription laws. The word quickly spread to Confederate regiments serving in Virginia and Tennessee, many believing the ruling invalidated the conscription laws. "Hence they draw the conclusion," wrote one North Carolina general to Vance, "that Enrolled conscripts will not only be justified in resisting the Law, but that those who have been held in service by the law, will not be arrested when they desert." Desertion was already a problem, especially in the regiments raised after the passage of the Conscription Act. The Fifty-Eighth, Sixtieth, Sixty-Second and Sixty-Fourth North Carolina Regiments were all mustered into service after April 1862, and all came from the foothill or mountain counties. Palmer's Fifty-Eighth Regiment was mustered into service in July 1862 and sent to East Tennessee, primarily guarding the passes between Cumberland Gap and Knoxville. By October 1, 1863, the regiment had 373 men listed as deserters or absent without leave and another 139 for whom the records are incomplete. By the end of the war, the Fifty-Eighth had a desertion rate of 34 percent. This was just ahead of the Sixtieth Regiment, which had a desertion rate of 33 percent. The records for the other two regiments are too incomplete to give an accurate percentage of deserters.[87]

Regiments from East Tennessee also struggled with desertion. Many of the regiments raised in East Tennessee in late 1861 through 1862 were part of the forces sent to Mississippi to reinforce the Vicksburg garrison. They battled the climate, bad water, mosquitoes and poor food, while also fighting the Federals at places like Chickasaw Bluff; Big Black Bridge, where the entire Sixtieth Tennessee surrendered; and the Siege of Vicksburg. When the East

Tennessee regiments were paroled after the capture of Vicksburg, they were ordered to reassemble at Jonesborough or Chattanooga. It was estimated that when the regiment was officially declared exchanged in September, half of the men failed to return to duty. "I am so sorry to say that our Vicksburg prisoners in East Tennessee are not reporting for duty. Our people who have been and are within the enemy's line are very disheartened," John C. Vaughn wrote to Jefferson Davis in October 1863. Many went back to their farms, while others took the Oath of Allegiance and joined the Federal army. Others simply scouted in the woods, attempting to avoid both armies, as well as the bushwhacking gangs that roamed the mountains.[88]

There were almost as many reasons for deserting as there were soldiers in the army. On May 19, 1863, at least twenty-five members of Company A, Thirty-Seventh North Carolina Troops, took their rifles and pay and went home to Ashe County. One officer of the regiment wrote that they deserted because of a disagreement concerning promotions within the company. Others were called home by their loved ones. Emsey Gragg slipped off from the Fifty-Eighth North Carolina in May 1863 and made his way back to Watauga County. The members of Cove Creek Baptist Church learned that "Brother Emsey Gragg had left his Regiment in the Army without leave, [and] agreed to send a committee to see Brother Gragg and report the facts at the next meeting." At that next meeting, the committee reported that Gragg's wife had sent him a letter, "stating that she and his family were suffering for the want of something to live on and he had come home to see what he could do." Gragg himself was at the October church meeting and "made acknowledgement for his act of desertion and promised to return to his Regiment as soon as he could," The members of the church agreed to suspend him. Gragg reappeared in the records of the Fifty-Eighth Regiment in January–February 1864, listed as present, but under arrest. He was reported as sick in May 1864 and then went over to the enemy, taking the Oath of Allegiance on June 14, 1864.[89]

From time to time, officers from various regiments were sent home to collect soldiers who were absent without leave, outright deserters or those not yet in service. William Walsh, Sixtieth Tennessee Infantry, sent his orderly sergeant back to Cocke County to look for men in early 1863. When the sergeant returned, he had twelve men in tow. Confederate regulation specified a reward of thirty dollars per deserter who was apprehended and delivered to the proper Confederate authorities. In June 1863, Ransom Hayes was paid for keeping eight deserters from the Fifty-Eighth North Carolina incarcerated in the Watauga County jail.[90]

However, a few returning officers, or the remnants of the militia, were not able to deal with the copious problems created by the deserters and conscript evaders. In North Carolina, Governor Vance established the Guard for Home Defense, known simply as the Home Guard, in July 1863. All white males between the ages of eighteen and fifty, including those exempt from conscription, like militia officers and justices of the peace, were enrolled in the Home Guard. While militia officers were elected by the people in the communities where they resided, Home Guard officers were appointed by the state. Each Western North Carolina county had at least one company and, in some cases, two companies. One company would often be on duty, looking for deserters, while the men in the other company were at home, tending to their farms. Tapped to lead the force was Yancey County's John W. McElroy. He was commissioned a brigadier general by the state and reported to Governor Vance. The governor's brother, Robert, had married McElroy's daughter prior to the war.[91]

John W. McElroy, the prewar commander of the Yancey County militia regiment, was chosen by Governor Vance to command the First Brigade, North Carolina Home Guard, in July 1863. *North Carolina Division of Archives and History.*

Vance's decision to form the Home Guard could not have come at a more opportune time. Violence was spreading across the mountains. In August 1863, a band came out of Johnson County and raided the Bethel community in Watauga County. The raiders attacked the farm of George Evans, holding Evans's wife hostage while they ransacked the home and took "four or five hundred dollars worth" of property, not only belonging to Evans but also to William Skiles, the missionary at the Valle Crucis Episcopal Church. Then they proceeded to the home of Paul Farthing, surrounding it and demanding his surrender. When Farthing refused to emerge, the mob started firing into the home. The ladies of the home repaired upstairs and started blowing horns, a predetermined signal that alerted their neighbors that help was needed. Upon hearing the warning, Thomas Farthing, Paul's older brother, grabbed his rifle and headed toward his brother's home. According to a friend, Thomas Farthing "unfortunately was discovered & fired upon by a guard stationed on the road side—two balls passing through his heart." After Farthing was killed, the attackers fled from the area. "The band was headed by a man by the name of Guy....They go in bands of 12 or 14." Blamed for the raid were the Guy brothers: Enoch, Canada and David. It appears that at least two of the brothers were later caught and executed for the crime. At some point, the Guys' father, Levi, was caught and hanged in Johnson County. There are two differing accounts of his hanging. John Preston Arthur wrote in 1915, "Some time later Levi Guy was captured by some of the Confederate Home Guard and hanged, although he protested that he had done nothing more than shelter his own sons when they came to his house for food and beds." An article on his grandson, David Franklin Guy, reports, "Mr. Guy's grandfather, Levi Guy, who had served during the Mexican War, was such an ardent Union supporter and so outspoken in his beliefs, that he incurred the enmity of those who had Southern sentiments and was eventually taken out and hung."[92]

Tracing the actions of the Home Guard in East Tennessee is a little more difficult. When Colonel Folk attacked the dissident camp at Fish Springs, he was accompanied by members of the "Johnson County Home Guard." Robert Crawford complained to Andrew Johnson that local Confederate supporters were organizing themselves into Home Guard companies. East Tennessee also had a Union Home Guard. Andrew Johnson was authorized to create a Guard for State Defense in May 1862. Like Western North Carolina, each Tennessee county composed a battalion or regiment. Johnson was further authorized to form ten regiments of infantry, with additional regiments of cavalry and artillery batteries by the U.S. War Department in March 1863, about the same time that the United States Congress passed its first Enrollment Act, also known as the Civil War Military Draft Act. The act stated that every male citizen between the ages of twenty and forty-five had to enroll. On September 13, 1863, Abraham Lincoln wrote to Johnson, encouraging him to "do your utmost to get every man you can, black and white, under arms at the very earliest moment, to guard roads, bridges, and trains, allowing all the better trained soldiers to" be redeployed to combat-ready forces.[93]

September 1863 brought a shift in the war in East Tennessee. Braxton Bragg, commanding the Army of Tennessee, concentrated Confederate forces from the surrounding department for a decisive blow against the Federal army venturing south from Chattanooga. Knoxville was abandoned, along with many of the men defending the railroad between Knoxville and Bristol. The only Confederate troops left in the area were a brigade at Cumberland Gap. That brigade, containing both the Sixty-Second and Sixty-Fourth North Carolina Regiments, surrendered on September 9. Federal cavalry and infantry, under the command of Ambrose Burnside, surged into Knoxville and much of the surrounding country. Burnside instructed his subordinates to use local loyal citizens to scout through the region, providing information on the activities of Confederates. With a large concentration of Federal soldiers close by, the partisan war intensified.[94]

Regular Federal soldiers spread out. A contingent of Ohio troops moved up the railroad, arriving in Jonesborough on September 5. After driving away Confederate cavalry, they succeeded in capturing a train. It was reported that two ladies were wounded during the mêlée. From Jonesborough, the Federals moved to Carter's Depot, demanding the surrender of the entrenched Confederate force guarding the railroad bridge. When Captain Hugh McClung refused to surrender, the Federals returned to Jonesborough. They wanted to continue back to Greeneville but found the trestle at Telford on fire. One Ohio regiment dug in at the old Embree

Federal forces under Ambrose Burnside poured through Cumberland Gap and headed toward Knoxville in September 1863. *From* Harper's Weekly.

house nearby. On September 6, Major William Stringfield moved his command from Carter's Station to Jonesborough but did not discover any Federals. A brigade of Confederate soldiers arrived on September 7, under the command of Brigadier General Alfred E. Jackson, unkindly known as "Mudwall" Jackson. The following day, they pushed toward Telford, driving the 100th Ohio back toward Limestone. At Limestone, the Ohio soldiers took shelter along the banks of Big Limestone Creek, in the blockhouse and the Gillespie house. Confederate forces surrounded the Federals, and when the Confederate artillery came into play, the Federals surrendered. Their losses were estimated at 20 killed, 30 wounded and 240 captured.[95]

When Burnside got news of the fighting, he dispatched Brigadier General James M. Shackleford with cavalry and artillery to assist. Commanding the Eighth Tennessee Cavalry (U.S.) was Colonel Samuel Patton, a former Washington County legislator, while the lieutenant colonel of the regiment, Andrew J. Brown, was once mayor of Jonesborough. It was the first time that regular Tennessee Unionists riding under the Stars and Stripes had entered the area. Once again, the Confederates were driven out of Jonesborough. On September 21 and 22, there was an effort to take Carter's Station. Federal artillery shelled the Confederate defenses and, by sending troops to cross at DeVault's and Taylor's Fords, managed to force the Confederates to withdraw to Zollicoffer. Small skirmishes frequently broke out in the area through the end of September.[96]

Conditions in Western North Carolina had worsened, Colonel James S. McElroy noted in a letter to Vance, since East Tennessee came under Federal control. Bands of Tories were forming, and McElroy had too few men to oppose them. Burnside reportedly ordered area post commanders to distribute surplus arms and ammunition to loyal citizens. "Good citizens in Madison County lay out [in the woods] every night in fear of their lives being taken," McElroy wrote. With the loss of the majority of East Tennessee, Confederate officials chose to create the Department of Western North Carolina. Brigadier General Robert B. Vance, brother to the governor, was assigned command. He had approximately five hundred soldiers in the department and was charged with protecting the border from Federal raiders. However, given the number of deserters, outliers and guerrillas between the borders, the area was virtually impossible for Confederate forces to defend.[97]

Federal recruiters swarmed throughout the area. In the Laurel section of Madison County, Joseph M. Squibb, a private in the Fourth Tennessee Infantry (U.S.), was present and recruiting for a new company in the Eighth

Left: Robert B. Vance was brother to Governor Zebulon Vance. *Library of Congress.*

Below: This Tennessee Historical Marker is near the site of the Battle of Limestone Station. *Author's collection.*

Tennessee Cavalry (U.S.). On September 1, seventy-four men joined a new regiment being raised from loyal Western North Carolina men. Only fifteen claimed their place of birth as Madison County, while it is possible that a few of those who claimed Yancey County as their birthplace actually lived in Madison at the time of the war. An additional twenty-four of the recruits were born in Tennessee or South Carolina. Several of these men were Confederate deserters. William Gentry, George Franklin, James Holland, Peter McCoy, Hackley Norton, Martin Norton and Roderick Norton were all conscripted into the Sixty-Fourth North Carolina in July 1862. Over the next seven months, they all deserted and headed back to Madison County. Upon joining the Union army, many of them were paid a $100 bounty. They received $25 not long after they enlisted, and the balance was due later. However, service in the Federal army did not appeal to many of these first recruits. Forty-five of the seventy-four men who joined on September 1 later deserted their commands. Only eighteen of the deserters returned, most in connection with an amnesty proclamation offered to deserters by Abraham Lincoln in the final days of the war.[98]

Many of these men probably knew that they were joining the Federal forces but were unsure to what regiment they would actually belong. Originally, these new recruits were assigned to the First North Carolina Mounted Infantry (U.S.). This regiment was ordered to report to Greeneville on October 16, 1863. When it was discovered that there was already a First North Carolina Volunteers in Federal service, the designation was changed to the Second North Carolina Mounted Infantry (U.S.). Appointed to command was James Albert Smith, formerly a captain in the Fifth Indiana Cavalry. The Fifth Indiana had chased Morgan's raiders in Kentucky in the summer of 1863, and it was the first regiment to enter Knoxville on September 1. Smith was appointed lieutenant colonel of the Second North Carolina Mounted Infantry on October 20. The new soldiers of Company E were positioned along the North Carolina–Tennessee border to help guide new recruits across the lines. Western North Carolina men poured into Greeneville to enlist in the Second throughout the month of September: 83 men filled out the ranks of Company A on September 15. Ten days later, 86 men joined Company B; another 83 men joined Company C the following day. On October 1, there were scores of men enlisting, some becoming part of existing companies, while others attempted to form new commands. All told, 575 men joined the Second North Carolina Mounted Infantry. Yet the regiment struggled and never completed its organization. Most of the companies never had captains.[99]

As Federal forces reached Johnson's Depot, "hundreds of Union men from Johnson and Carter Counties...greeted them with the greatest demonstrations of joy" imaginable. Roderick Butler, a Johnson County judge and representative in the Tennessee General Assembly, along with Carter County sheriff John K. Miller, gained permission from Andrew Johnson to raise a new regiment. Butler ran the following advertisement in local newspapers:

> *Rally East Tennesseans and North Carolinians!*
>
> *By permission of Major General A.P. Burnside, I am raising a regiment of infantry for the service of the United States, and I appeal to the Union men of the mountains of Tennessee and North Carolina to come forth immediately. Good arms and clothing will be furnished you immediately. Your bounties of money and land will be promptly paid.*[100]

The new regiment was originally designated the Twelfth Tennessee Cavalry (U.S.), but the designation was speedily changed to the Thirteenth Tennessee Cavalry (U.S.). Enrollment was soon underway. A handful had previously enlisted in the regiment in Kentucky, but on September 20, several dozen men joined Company F in Carter County. More enlisted the following day in Carter and Greene Counties, but the bulk of the regiment joined the ranks between September 22 and September 24, not only in Carter and Greene Counties but in Johnson and Washington as well. As Federal forces fell back toward Greeneville, the recruits also fell back. According to veterans, writing decades after the war, the new men had been fed, given frying pans and armed with "some old Springfield rifles." Yet on the night of September 30, they retreated into the darkness. "Rumors of fighting, verified by the sound of musketry in our rear, was a new experience to most of us....[W]e were receiving 'the baptism of fire'; but we reached Bull's Gap in safety, and with no loss except frying pans and perhaps a few muskets that some of us threw away to accelerate our speed." Enrollment of new soldiers shifted to Knox and Cocke Counties. At Strawberry Plains, between October 28 and November 8, nine new companies were legitimately mustered into the Thirteenth Tennessee Cavalry, and John Miller officially became colonel, with Butler as lieutenant colonel. Much to the chagrin of many who thought Burnside's arrival in East Tennessee promised the liberation of the area from the hated Confederates, the Thirteenth Tennessee marched toward

Camp Nelson in Kentucky at the end of November to be trained and properly equipped.[101]

A struggle for the mountains was being waged on a small scale as the trees turned to their glorious autumn shades of yellow, gold, red and crimson. Confederate forces swept through the Laurel section of Madison County on October 1, capturing a recruiter and twelve men trying to make their way into Tennessee. At the same time, a group of Virginia deserters masquerading as members of "Williams' Virginia Cavalry" were corralled and captured in Watauga County. They were two days beyond Asheville when the alarm was raised. Major John Woodfin set out with twenty-five men and captured thirty-six. The Virginia soldiers were sent to Camp Vance in Burke County, and Woodfin returned a hero for having "returned 36 soldiers to duty and rid the country of a dangerous band of *free dealers* in horse flesh." On October 3, Confederate forces began moving toward Bull's Gap, in Hawkins County, northwest of Greeneville. Their goal was to disrupt Union communications and logistics, with hopes of also capturing portions of the East Tennessee and Virginia Railroad. A fairly heated skirmish was fought at Blue Springs, with the Federals retreating. Skirmishing went on for several days. On October 10, Federal and Confederate forces clashed at Bull's Gap. While the Confederates tenuously held their lines, they retreated under the cover of darkness that night, eventually moving back into the

Daniel Ellis carried mail to and from the members of the Thirteenth Tennessee Cavalry. *From* The Thrilling Adventures of Daniel Ellis.

defensive works at Bristol. There was another skirmish in Laurel sometime around October 12. Robert V. Blackstock wrote his friend Governor Vance of the details: Captain Roberts took several men into the Laurel area and "killed one and wounded three, all Tories from Buncombe. Ingle, the one killed, lived on Big Ivy; had run away, went to the Yankees, got a companion to raise a company; he was killed running, of course."[102]

Someone, possibly Federal brigadier general Orlando B. Willcox, decided that a foray into North Carolina was warranted. Recruiting had gone well the first of September, and perhaps a force in Madison County would encourage others to cross the lines and join the Federal army. Pegged to undertake the operation was Lieutenant Colonel James A. Smith and his men from the Second North Carolina Mounted Infantry (U.S.). On October 16, Smith marched the un-mounted men into Warm Springs. Carrie Rumbough had arrived in Warm Springs in 1862, a refugee from East Tennessee, and was managing the hotel. According to local history, on hearing of the approach of the Federals, she and a "Faithful negro maid" burned one of the bridges over the French Broad River. When the Federals arrived, the heights north of town were fortified, while soldiers occupied the hotel and other buildings.[103]

Robert Vance had a small force a few miles away in Marshall. Vance ordered Colonel Allen, of the Sixty-Fourth North Carolina, to take an undisclosed number of Confederate soldiers and link up with the Fourteenth North Carolina Cavalry Battalion under the command of Major John Woodfin to drive the Federals out of Warm Springs. The Federals learned of the attack the night before yet chose to dig in and fight. When Federals captured some of the Confederate pickets, Vance scaled back the operation, unsure exactly what he was facing. On the morning of October 20, Allen and Woodfin led their men toward Warm Springs. The Federals had their forces spread out. One group was posted along Spring Creek. Another company was posted higher, overlooking the road, while members of a third company positioned themselves in the hotel. "We had some fighters with us, but we also had some too timid to fire a gun," John Pickens, a private in the Second North Carolina, wrote decades after the war. Allen went ahead with a group of eleven others, including Woodfin and William Henry, scouting the Federal position. The Confederates quickly captured the first Federal line or "outpost" and moved north. Allen noted that the bridge was torn up, and here, a "sharp fight ensued." After a skirmish of undetermined length, Confederate forces began falling back. Allen, Woodfin and several privates were cut off from the rest of the command. Their only avenue of escape was to scale an "almost perpendicular" mountain to the north. Woodfin was seen to fall from his horse, pierced by two balls, about the time they started up the mountain. Federal forces also suffered several losses. Lieutenant James Grace, adjutant of the Second North Carolina, was seen fleeing the field. Several soldiers tracked him down, finding his lifeless form propped up against a peach tree. He had been shot in the throat. Apparently, Grace was a prewar friend of Carrie Rumbough, and she clipped a lock of his hair before she and two slaves buried him nearby.[104]

Losses on either side are unknown. It is not even clear just what force Allen was commanding. Most of the Sixty-Fourth North Carolina had been captured a couple of weeks earlier at Cumberland Gap. The remnants were ordered to re-form in neighboring Haywood County. When citizens from Asheville arrived the next day under a flag of truce to recover Woodfin's body, they found no Federal soldiers. Woodfin had been stripped of his watch and uniform. Allen and several others escaped up the mountain, becoming separated. According to his biographer, Allen was forced to abandon his horse and his boots, keeping to the "rugged ledges of the mountains" and wading "deep streams." Two nights after the skirmish, he spotted a fire and "cautiously moved near." Federal soldiers crowded around the fire. "One of them was upon a stump crowing like a rooster," rejoicing over a Confederate soldier at home on sick leave whom they had dragged out of his father's home and killed. "Colonel Allen pulled his revolver, and at the report the human rooster fell in the fire and others took to the bush." Allen reached the Confederate lines in Marshall the following day.[105]

While the citizens tasked with the mournful occupation of retrieving Woodfin's body claimed they found no Federals, Union forces were still in the area. The hotel in Warm Springs was sacked, and the men of the Second North Carolina "carried off negroes, horses, bed clothing, wearing clothing, table ware, in fact everything portable....It is said that they did not leave a single horse on Spring Creek," the *Asheville News* reported a few weeks later. Allen went as far as to claim that the hooligans "killed and scalped Major Holcomb and James Arrington, who were Southern soldiers but then at home; shot down old James Garrett at his gate, aged seventy years...went to William Pecks...aged seventy-two, took his shoes and compelled him to go over to his plantation in the cold and dark in his bare feet and give them all his horses." The *Asheville News* wrote that the homes of Barnard, Blair, Patton, Garrett, Fagg and Askew were all robbed. John McElroy wrote to Governor Vance that "the Tories...fired on our pickets yesterday" in Yancey County and "probably burned Samuel Bakers' house in Mitchell County last. If that is the case, give us leave to burn up that whole Tory region." McElroy believed he would soon have six hundred troops in the Toe River Valley and was contemplating a move into Tennessee to reclaim stolen horses.[106]

Robert Vance was more than determined to drive the Unionists out of northern Madison County. On October 25, he sent eighty members of the Twenty-Fifth North Carolina, aided by twenty members of the Haywood County Home Guard, toward Warm Springs. Lieutenant Colonel Samuel C. Bryson commanded the small group. About daylight, they moved in to attack:

> *Instead of finding a picket at his outpost, I found him drawn up in line of battle waiting to receive me, he having discovered the plan, from all accounts, early the night before. When I made the attack, although he numbered, as was afterwards ascertained, about 400 in line, I charged him and completely routed him from his position, and drove him beyond the field. A second time coming up, showed the same result. A third time they reinforced and came. With this force my little band struggled for some time successfully, but seeing that we were completely overwhelmed in point of numbers, I gave the order to fall back, which most of the men did in good order....In a hand to hand encounter Sergeant Collins rushed forward and sacrificed his own life to save mine. Maj. Rhea and a portion of his militia fought well, but the conduct of the others was not very good.*

Bryson placed his losses at four killed, five wounded. Federal losses were reported as four killed and eight wounded. Soon thereafter, Smith pulled his men back into Tennessee, moving closer to Greeneville.[107]

It was later widely claimed that the Unionist occupation in Warm Springs was led by George W. Kirk. While he probably was present, his name does not appear on letters or records from October through December 1863. Although the Second North Carolina might have gained some supplies, the mission to recruit men while in Warm Springs was, overall, a disaster. Only one man joined the Federal ranks. There were a few who enrolled in the regiment on November 1 in Cumberland Gap, Knoxville or Bull's Gap. In those same two months, October and November 1863, at least sixty-one men were absent without leave or declared deserters. Added to this were a handful of men listed as killed or captured, and the Warm Springs raid was a Unionist loss.[108]

Robert Vance pushed his forces across the state line and into Tennessee. He reported to his brother on November 12 that he had "raided Cocke County and part of Greene pretty thoroughly." He had "liberated" some eight hundred hogs, some horses and an undisclosed number of cattle. On November 11, a portion of his command was attacked and lost one hundred of the hogs. Five miles from Newport, Vance met a portion of the Unionists and drove "the enemy back several hundred yards," losing two wounded in the process.[109]

Vance was working in conjunction with Confederate forces under Lieutenant General James Longstreet. In September 1863, Longstreet moved two of his divisions from Virginia to Georgia and played a decisive role in the defeat of Federal forces at the Battle of Chickamauga. Yet the Confederates wasted an opportunity to deal a more decisive blow, and the Federals retreated back into Chattanooga. Longstreet clashed with his superior, Braxton Bragg. With Burnside in Knoxville, Bragg seized the opportunity to rid himself of Longstreet. On November 3, Longstreet was ordered to take his men and drive the Federals out of Knoxville and East Tennessee. Due to poor rail logistics, Longstreet did not arrive in the area until November 12. Burnside slowly withdrew his force back toward Knoxville, hoping reinforcements would soon arrive. Longstreet ordered his infantry and artillery to dig in to the north and west, while sending his cavalry to the northeast. At the same time, Federals were strengthening their defenses. However, Confederate forces did not have enough men to completely shut off the city from outside supply lines. A faulty map left open supply routes to the south, and Unionists in Sevier and Jefferson Counties sent supplies to the Federal soldiers in Knoxville. When pressured by Bragg, Longstreet finally ordered an attack on Fort Sanders on November 29, an attack that failed. The fight lasted twenty minutes and cost the Confederates 813 in dead, wounded and captured. With word that Federal reinforcements were near, Longstreet began to move toward the northeast on December 3. His men camped in and around Bull's Gap until April 1864. One of Longstreet's staff officers noted in late 1863, "In east Tennessee the people are about equally divided and there rages a real civil war, which causes great misery."[110]

Confederates spread out of the area. Longstreet sent much of his cavalry to Sevier and Jefferson Counties to protect his foraging details. A member of the Fourth Alabama Infantry recalled that their commissary wagons were kept busy "between the Holston and French Broad Rivers, collecting supplies." These foraging details never lacked volunteers. It was an opportunity to break the boredom of winter camp life. The details "would generally return with a supply of provisions to last them for some time." A private in the Fifteenth Alabama recalled it differently: "The winter of

Fort Sanders was unsuccessfully attacked by Longstreet's troops in November 1863. *Library of Congress.*

'63–64 at Morristown, Tenn., was peculiarly hard. We had no huts, rations were scant and poor, as were blankets, clothing and shoes. We did not get a mail for three months. Plug tobacco could not be had." A local historian wrote that members of the Ninth Georgia Battalion were encamped next to the mill in the Patterson community of Caldwell County. One local resident wrote to Governor Vance that Longstreet's men had "come down through McDowell, Burke & Caldwell [Counties] & have nearly consumed all the grain they could pick up….What are poor day laborers to do for bread when every crib in the land is depleted to the lowest possible standard….I see a dark day ahead for the poor sons of toil and in fact for us all unless some unforseen good luck should happen." It was not only Longstreet's command out foraging. Portions of Thomas's Legion moved through the Laurel community in the dead of winter, looking for supplies, while also capturing a few dissidents along the way.[111]

James Longstreet commanded a corps in the Army of Northern Virginia. Many of his troops spent the winter of 1863–64 in East Tennessee. *Library of Congress.*

In October, the Thirty-Fourth Battalion, Virginia Cavalry, under the command of Lieutenant Colonel Vincent Witcher, moved into East Tennessee. Witcher himself was apparently absent, at least part of the time attending to matters in Bristol and Christiansburg. The Thirty-Fourth Battalion, Virginia Cavalry, had a good reputation prior to its arrival in the area. Even Major General J.E.B. Stuart had commented on the men's bravery at Gettysburg. Yet Witcher's command also had somewhat of a dubious standing. The *Bristol Gazette* reported in early 1864 the capture of a Yankee in Lee County accused of rape. It was the prayer of the editor of the *Richmond Sentinel* that the man "may fall into the hands of Colonel Witcher." Like several other Confederate commands during the war, the Thirty-Fourth Virginia appears to have been ordered to make a sweep through Carter and Johnson Counties.[112]

Wilkes County native John Q.A. Bryan spent the first part of November recruiting in Wilkes County, largely in the Trap Hill section. He gathered more than fifty new recruits for the Tenth Tennessee Cavalry (U.S.), and soon they were making their way through the mountains toward Knoxville. After they had traveled all night, on the morning of November 19, 1863, the group could be found at the home of Dr. David Bell. Born in Ireland, Bell had moved his family to Carter County in the 1850s. The Bells were affluent slave owners and pronounced Unionists.[113]

From out of nowhere, elements of the Thirty-Fourth Battalion, Virginia Cavalry, arrived on the scene. The battalion spent its first night near Carter's Depot, then moved up Buffalo Creek to Greasy Cove, supposedly killing "several men." These were being led by local guides, including Nathaniel Brown, Alfred Leslie, William Peoples and Madison Peoples. As the mounted troops came into view, the Unionists broke for the brush. The majority escaped, and the Confederates were able to capture only seven. All seven were killed. Calvin Cartrel was shot and then his brains "knocked…out"; John Sparks "was shot in the head…which completely tore the top of his head off, leaving his brains perfectly exposed"; William Royal was shot at least once, and then a "fence-stake" was used to "beat his head into the earth"; Elijah Gentry was shot and killed instantly; Jacob Lyons was shot and fell into a creek; B. Blackburn was shot in the shoulder, then beaten to death; and Preston Prewett was shot and, while imploring his captors to send word of his demise, had his brains knocked "out with the butts of their guns." Others were wounded. Jacob Pruitt sought a pension after the war for wounds sustained in the attack. A doctor testified that Pruitt was shot near the Bell home, "the ball having entered his body on the left side of spinal column, passing out through the stomach about one half of an inch above the navel." John W. Brooks was shot in the knee but hid behind a log and escaped death. Bryan was reported to have escaped, killing a soldier who pursued him. Just how many others were wounded and escaped is unknown.[114]

Returning to the home, James Bell was dragged outside. His wife followed and attempted to intercede on Bell's behalf. The soldiers drove her back in the house, "threatening to shoot her if she offered to speak again in his behalf." According to an article written a few months later, Bell was "forced to lay his head on a chunk in the road, and with stones and clubs they *beat his brains out.* They took some of the blood and brains and *rubbed them under his wife's nose, cursing her, and telling her to smell them!*" Next, the band turned its attention to the home. Unionist William Sparks was sick and had been taken in to recover by the Bell family. One account states that when the attack began, he was secreted in the basement by slipping through a raised plank in the kitchen floor. Soldiers piled clothes on the floor and attempted to set them on fire. When that failed, they added a straw bed to the mix. As the soldiers vacated the house, Sparks was able to escape. Another account states that Sparks was given a dress and bonnet to wear and slipped out of the cellar undetected. Those killed were buried close by the house.[115]

While Witcher's Thirty-Fourth Virginia has traditionally been blamed for the Limestone Cove Massacre, there is not any real proof that those men were involved in the horrific incident. Unlike the Shelton Laurel events at the beginning of the year, there does not seem to be a paper trail or investigation into the deaths of these Unionists attempting to pass through the lines and into Federal service. There was another Witcher, James, who commanded the Sullivan County Reserves, roaming about the area. However, James Witcher probably did not command four hundred men.

A Tennessee Historical Marker locates the possible burial site of those killed by Witcher's Cavalry in late 1863. *Author's collection.*

Many considered the Cherokee Indians of Thomas's Legion the most dreaded Confederate soldiers in East Tennessee. *From* The Thrilling Adventures of Daniel Ellis.

While some group was trying to curtail the flow of refugees and recruits for the Union army coursing through Carter and Johnson Counties, there were several skirmishes between local forces in Cocke and Sevier Counties. Both Thomas and Vance were ordered to link up with Longstreet's command. Robert Vance had actually been relieved of command on November 18 but, for some unknown reason, stayed in the field with his troops. Longstreet was attempting to gain authority over the troops in Western North Carolina, hoping to augment his own command. Instead, Thomas and Vance made their own independent incursions into East Tennessee. Around December 8, Thomas, with two hundred men, rode into Sevierville. Some of his men captured earlier were released from the local jail, and they captured several Federal soldiers and members of the local Unionist Home Guard. Thomas then returned to Gatlinburg, expressing to locals that he intended to spend the winter. Burnside learned of the raid and sent the Fifteenth Pennsylvania Cavalry from Knoxville toward Gatlinburg. The Federals divided their forces. The main force would take a steep trail across Cove Mountain toward Thomas's rear, while a smaller force advanced along the main road. Local scouts guided the main force across the mountain under the cover of darkness. At daybreak on December 10, the Federals launched their attack, quickly surprising the Confederate pickets. Thomas had chosen his camp well. The Federals were forced to dismount as Cherokees fired down on them from the hillside. Each crack of a rifle was followed by a war whoop. The skirmishing lasted for several hours, and the Confederates eventually withdrew. Confederate losses are unknown, although it was reported that the Federals captured "16 horses, 18 muskets, 2 boxes of ammunition, several bushels of salt, meal, dried fruit," along with several Cherokee women. The camp was burned and the Federals moved back toward Knoxville. Colonel Thomas wrote about the skirmish, stating that two of his men had been wounded in the affair: "The enemy have at least been taught that while we hold the Smoky Mountains of Western N. Carolina…the adjacent portions of East Tennessee are hard to subjugate."[116]

Toward the end of December, Robert Vance launched his own raid. He found a group of Tories, estimated to be three hundred strong, encamped on the head of Cosby Creek in Cocke County. Vance, whose force reportedly consisted of a few regulars, Home Guard companies from Haywood and Henderson Counties, charged the dissidents. Three were killed, three wounded and six to eight captured, along with all of the camp equipment. Confederate losses were not reported. "Gen. Vance says veteran troops never acted more gallantly," the *Asheville News* reported.[117]

The officers in Thomas's Legion: 1. Colonel William H. Thomas 2. Colonel James R. Love 3. Major William W. Stringfield 4. Captain James W. Cooper 5. Lieutenant Robert T. Conley 6. Lieutenant David K. Collins 7. Lieutenant James Conley 8. Lieutenant William T. Welsh. *North Carolina Division of Archives and History.*

For those men and women living along the North Carolina–Tennessee border, 1863 had been a long, trying year. Many of their loved ones were dead, in prison or forced to hide out in the caves and hollows that dotted the region. Many other families had been completely displaced, forced to flee north or farther south, trying to escape the war as it swirled around the mountains and streams that they called home. While many hoped for peace, 1864 would bring only more bloodshed and heartache.

4

1864

"Time Will Suffice to Tell You of All the Horrors to Which They Are Exposed"

Despite being ordered to report for a new assignment, Robert Vance refused to relinquish field command. His replacement was Colonel John B. Palmer. After leading the Fifty-Eighth North Carolina out of the Tar Heel State, Palmer's men spent thirteen months guarding the passes between Cumberland Gap and Knoxville. When Bragg drew down the Confederate regiments from East Tennessee, the Fifty-Eighth Regiment set off for Chickamauga. The regiment was involved on day two of the battle there, helping drive the Federal defenders from Snodgrass Hill. Palmer was wounded in the action and returned to Western North Carolina to recover. There were several voices advocating for Palmer's promotion to brigadier general at the time that he was assigned to command the district of Western North Carolina.[118]

Reports were flowing into Union headquarters in Knoxville regarding raids against citizens in Cocke County. First on the list of reported offenders was a group of one hundred men under a Captain Rumbough. They considered themselves "freebooters" and had robbed locals of "horses, cattle, grain, clothing, bedding, and every other species of household furniture." Several homes had been burned, and men had been hanged in attempts to force disclosure of money. There was a Reverend Kelly whose ears had been cut off, and then he was beaten to death. Robert Cody was also killed. Two Federal soldiers home on parole were dragged outside and shot, but they apparently survived. David Hamed, who had sons in the Union army, was also paid a visit by these thugs. Hamed was "robbed…of every bushel of corn, every piece of meat, every horse, cow, hog, and sheep; [they] also stripped him of his clothing, robbed his house of all manner of furniture, and then outraged his daughters in his presence. Passing on to his daughter who was sick upon her bed, with an infant hours old, they stripped the covering off her, and left her exposed until she died."[119]

Vance launched another raid on January 8. His force consisted of a section of artillery, 100 infantrymen and 375 cavalry riders. They passed through Waynesville and Quallatown, where portions of Thomas's Legion joined the group. In Tennessee, Thomas remained at Gatlinburg with the artillery, while Vance proceeded to Sevierville with 180 cavalrymen. On January 13, Confederates captured seventeen Federal wagons sent out from Knoxville to collect forage. From Gatlinburg, Vance moved toward Newport, stopping near Schultz's Mill to feed his horses. A portion of Thomas's command, under Lieutenant Colonel James L. Henry, had been ordered to Schultz's Mill to reinforce Vance's command. Henry, however, chose to disregard these orders. The Fifteenth Pennsylvania Cavalry, camped on the French Broad River, set out in pursuit the following day. Portions of the Tenth Ohio Cavalry accompanied the Pennsylvanians, creating a combined force of 200 troopers. After covering thirty miles, the Federal cavalry found the Confederates preparing to advance. Vance had not thrown out any type of rear guard, and the Federals were able to move within one hundred yards before being detected. "I immediately charged them in column of fours," the Federal commanding officer wrote, "routing their entire command, which fled in the utmost disorder, throwing away their guns, belts, blankets, saddle-bags, &c." The Federals claimed to have captured 52 men, 150 horses, over one hundred arms and "a fine ambulance filled with medical stores," along with bacon, salt and meal. Vance was imprisoned at Fort Delaware, only to be released a month before the war ended. John B. Palmer's first real role as department commander was to write a report detailing the capture of Robert Vance.[120]

A few months later, an article appeared in North Carolina newspapers concerning the capture of some of Thomas's men, possibly at one of the skirmishes in or near Sevierville. The Cherokee prisoners, held in Knoxville, were "flattered and feasted, big talks held, and magnificent promises made, if they would abandon the Confederacy and join the Lincoln government." The Cherokee were promised $5,000 in gold if they would bring in the scalp of William Holland Thomas. After consulting for a time, they agreed and were released. They returned to the Smokies, "sought the camp of their Chief, told him all, and have ever since been on the war-path—*after the Yankee scalps!*" It is believed that at this time, Thomas organized a "Life Guard," twenty Cherokees who "were constantly with him as protection to his person against robbers."[121]

There were numerous small incidents in the mountains in January and February. William Walker, commander of Walker's Battalion, Thomas's Legion, was sick at home in Cherokee County when a knock at the door summoned him. Dissidents had surrounded the house, and as Walker opened the door, he was shot and killed. Other elements of Thomas's Legion were bound for Indian Creek in Washington County. A small skirmish between them and a band of dissidents killed one of the latter by the name of Pritchard. Daniel Ellis was still piloting disgruntled residents through the mountains, but Longstreet's position forced Ellis to change his route. He was now traveling through Greasy Cove and Flag Pond, thus skirting the northern sections of the Toe River Valley, to reach the Laurel community in Madison County. From there, his route turned north toward Knoxville. One newspaper reported that a group of these dissidents was surprised in Carter County on the eve of their journey. The article states that five of the seventeen were "dispatched" and three captured. Those three were later seen being escorted "into Bristol tied together with ropes."[122]

Federal foraging parties moved into Cocke and Sevier Counties in mid-January. Cavalry found the Dutch Bottoms and Irish Bottoms communities so stripped of forage that "a division of cavalry could not subsist longer than three days." The main Federal party stayed in the Sevierville area. There were forays into Cocke County and a skirmish near Newport that secured sixteen Confederate prisoners and three thousand bushels of corn.[123]

In January and February, especially in the Madison-Cocke-Sevier County area, the war quickly drifted across state borders. Palmer informed Longstreet that on January 25, three hundred Confederate cavalrymen were sweeping toward Newport. Longstreet wanted them to range as far as Sevierville. Two days later, the two sides clashed four miles east of Sevierville on the East Fork of the Pigeon River. Federal cavalrymen were attempting to disrupt Confederate foraging details. Fighting broke out on January 26 at Fair Garden. Confederate cavalry drove back Federal troops, and the next day, Federal forces counterattacked. In the end, Confederate forces were pushed back, losing two cannons and more than one hundred men as prisoners. Federal losses were approximately seventy. When Longstreet sent reinforcements on January 28, the Federals withdrew.[124]

A few days later, word arrived that Thomas's command was encamped near Quallatown in Jackson County. Thomas and his "savages" had earned quite a reputation. The area Federal cavalry commander wrote that Thomas's men "had become a terror to the Union people of East Tennessee and the borders of North Carolina from the atrocities they were daily perpetrating." After the war, another Federal soldier wrote that Thomas's Legion had committed "many of the most barbarous atrocities" in the border area. "They were a kind of independent 'flying command,' to whom was assigned the commission of deeds that cowardly rebels desired to have done but dared not perform." Orders soon directed the Fourteenth Illinois Cavalry, with forty to fifty guides and two pieces of artillery, to slip through the mountains and strike Thomas. The Fourteenth Illinois departed on January 31. Washington Sanford, a junior officer in the Illinois regiment, left a vivid description of crossing the mountains. At times, troopers were forced to dismount and lead their horses. It "required great care and skill to prevent their going over yawning precipices that verged our mountain path," Sanford wrote many years later. The cavalry made camp that night after covering thirteen miles. Rain fell in torrents, accompanied by "a mighty wind, which moaned and roared through the mountain forests, caves and gorges, making weird music not well calculated to soothe gentle slumber." After another day of travel, the Federals were in position and surprised the Confederate camp on the morning of February 2. The few accounts of this skirmish present vastly varied stories. Governor Vance received a letter stating the Cherokees "fought nobly, under the surprise, until their ammunition failed." They then withdrew from the contest. Yet a column in the *Asheville News* painted a different picture: "Col. Thomas' Indians bushwhacked them so unmercifully that they turned at that point and hurriedly retreated....The dead they left where they fell." Sanford wrote that the victory belonged to the Federals, who, after burying the dead, started back over the mountain with their wounded and prisoners.[125]

Residents in Hendersonville reported hearing the sound of cannons off in the distant mountains. Colonel Palmer was able to report that the Federals had departed by February 8, and he himself traveled to inspect the area, returning to Asheville by February 12. Palmer was probably in the saddle again a week later. Rumors reached him that George W. Kirk was possibly in Shelton Laurel. Palmer left a small force in Marshall, under the command of Lieutenant Colonel Bryan McDowell, and moved the rest of his force into the area. Palmer's sweep, reportedly with members of the Eighteenth Mississippi, remains largely undocumented. The other column under McDowell had orders to cross over the Big Laurel in support of

Palmer's operations. Forty of his own men, along with twenty from the Sixty-Fourth North Carolina, set out on a "two day scout." One officer wrote of the exercise:

> *We made a forced march and about 3:30 p.m. the enemy began to bushwhack us.... We camped that night in a little valley between three hills. In the meantime we had learned that Kirk's whole command was there, so we naturally expected a fight the next morning and we got it....* [J]*ust as day began to dawn the firing commenced,* [and] [i]*n a short time we were on top of one of the hills....Kirk's command was not in a body but were in every direction and had good long range rifles. We were not as well armed as they were, but the boys put in good time. Just at the foot of the hill there was a little group gathered that was pouring shot into us....* [W]*e of the Sixty-fourth...made a charge and when* [we were] *about half way...the enemy...took to the woods.... We then had to climb the hill...under heavy fire from all directions except...our lines. When we had gotten back we found Lieutenant-Colonel McDowell shot through the arm and the men out of ammunition. The next thing was to get out, which we did very nicely by making a charge both ways. When they ran we marched out, having a long trip up a mountain. The enemy fired many shots, but we being out of ammunition, had to take it quietly. However, we lost only two killed and four wounded, and returned to Marshall.*[126]

George W. Kirk was making headlines along the border region, but he disappeared from the records of the Eighth Tennessee Cavalry (U.S.) sometime in the summer of 1863. Those records state that Kirk was absent, "Acting Major in the 1 North Carolina Regt Vols." He does not reappear until February 1864. On the thirteenth, Major General Schofield authorized Kirk to raise a new "regiment of troops in the Eastern part of Tennessee and western part of North Carolina." The new regiment was to be mustered in as infantry, but Kirk could mount a portion of his men "upon private or captured horses." Schofield closed by christening the new regiment the Third North Carolina Mounted Infantry (U.S.).[127]

Kirk had been recruiting for the Second North Carolina Mounted Infantry (U.S.) throughout the mountain region. From period correspondence, it seems Kirk was a recruiter and not attached to any regiment between October 1863 and February 1864. Now, however, he had permission to raise his own regiment, and he appeared to be trying to siphon off the men he had recruited for the Second in order to bolster his new Third Regiment.

Adjutant Charles Wilson wrote to the assistant adjutant general in Knoxville about the matter. Wilson felt the recruits in Knoxville would be better employed in filling the ranks of the Second, instead of in trying to form a new regiment. Although he did not have the proof at hand, Wilson believed that there was enough evidence against Kirk to prevent him "from ever holding a commission in the Union army….I consider him unworthy of a position in the Federal ranks or even among men and from what I can learn…he is with out honor or respect." Yet the Second North Carolina was having problems of its own. In a letter dated two weeks prior to Wilson's, Brigadier General Theophilus Garrard wrote to Schofield's headquarters, complaining that the Second had but 220 men present, who were without discipline and were "of but little value." Wilson wrote on behalf of Lieutenant Colonel James Smith, who was absent, and went on to resign in June 1864.[128]

On March 2, the "notorious Kirk" and thirty-five men rode into the Flag Pond community in Washington County. A few days earlier, Lieutenant John J. Duck, Sixty-Fourth North Carolina Troops, had been sent with a detachment of twelve men to garrison the area. Their job was probably to watch the local roads and look for dissidents attempting to cross over the mountain. Kirk's men "dashed" toward the group, killing one and capturing several more, all of whom they promptly executed. One of the lot, Reuben Woodward, a private in the Sixty-Fourth, struggled for life for a couple of hours before one of Kirk's band put a gun to his head and "blew his brains out." Duck himself escaped with the others. Kirk's group then went to the Blankenship house and killed Presley Blankenship and his son Lafayette. After stripping the dead, they took Blankenship's horses and hitched them to his wagon. They then loaded the contents of the house and farm into the wagon, even driving off his cows. Later, this event would be dubbed the Indian Creek Massacre.[129]

Other small events kept mountain citizens wary. About the same time that Kirk was thought to be in Flag Pond, he was also reported to be skirmishing with the Yancey County Home Guard under Samuel Byrd Sr. The Home Guard reportedly killed one and wounded two or three of Kirk's bunch, while two of their own were slightly wounded. On March 31, in Washington County, John Bennett, a deserter from the Thirteenth Tennessee Cavalry (U.S.), was captured by local forces and sent to prison, and about the first of April, the remnants of the Sixty-Fourth North Carolina were ordered from Madison County to Flat Rock in Henderson County. Their mission was to disperse a band of robbers. One resident along the North Toe River was concerned that the Tories would destroy the Cranberry Iron Works.

It "would be an immense loss," he wrote Governor Vance. At the same time, the writer believed that the workers at the ironworks that were being constructed by "Mr. Jones," probably those located at Linville Falls, should be armed, "and the works allowed to have military drills each day."[130]

Even if there was no direct link or evidence of his presence, Kirk was often blamed for any bloodletting that occurred in the North Carolina mountains. Kirk is often believed to be the impetus behind an invasion into Yancey County in April 1864, although there is no proof.

"The tories, several hundred strong, occupied the town of Burnsville, last week," the *Asheville News* reported on April 21. According to a letter from John W. McElroy to Governor Vance, a group of fifty local women stormed the town on April 9. They proceeded to a warehouse, taking "sixty bushels of Government wheat." This wheat was most likely a part of the produce collected for the tax-in-kind program. Each farmer had to pay a certain amount of tax in foodstuffs. On the following day, Montreval Ray, a deserter from the Confederate army, led seventy-five dissidents into town. Ray had volunteered to serve one year in the Sixteenth North Carolina State Troops. A year to the day later, he and a couple of others deserted and headed home. Ray's band broke into a local building and stole weapons and ammunition intended for the Home Guard. They then shot the local Confederate enrolling officer in the arm, but he was able to escape. Next, they broke into Broyles's store and "carried off the contents." Another correspondent to Vance related how the dissidents dragged out Milton Penland under the pretext of hanging him if he would not surrender beeves, bacon and wheat. Penland did eventually comply with their demands.[131]

Palmer was not in Western North Carolina at the time. Instead, he was in Richmond reporting on the deteriorating conditions in Western North Carolina. As he returned to the area, word reached him concerning the dramatic events unfolding in Burnsville. He took the majority of his force, the five companies he had in Asheville and a single piece of artillery, and entered Yancey County. The exact details of the ensuing skirmish are not known, but Palmer apparently placed his cannon on a hill overlooking the town, fired a couple of rounds and then ordered his men to charge. Mont Ray escaped, as did many others, but Palmer succeeded in capturing over a dozen men. McElroy's old house in Burnsville was, according to local lore, used as a hospital for the wounded from both sides. Possibly captured was Amos Ray, Montreval's father. In retaliation for the property that had been destroyed, Palmer ordered the burning of the Burnsville store owned by Amos Ray and soon returned to Asheville with his prisoners.[132]

"The county is gone," McElroy lamented to Vance in a letter detailing the deplorable circumstances found in the area. Local citizens refused to help defend against the raiders and ran off when Ray's band first appeared. "It has got to be impossible to get any man out of there unless he is dragged out, with but few exceptions." At the time of the Burnsville Raid, McElroy's headquarters were at Mars Hill, in Madison County. He stated that he only had one hundred men with him, guarding against Kirk's forays and against the dissidents in Laurel. "[T]o call out any more home guards at this time is only certain destruction," McElroy believed. And then there was the problem with conscription. "Swarms of men liable to conscription are gone to the tories or to the Yankees," McElroy complained, adding that the work of the Conscription officers was "a very tyrannical course….[I]f they are called upon to do a little home-guard service, they at once apply for a writ of habeas corpus and get off….This emboldens the tories, and they are now largely recruited by conscript renegades and very soon it is possible our country may be full of Yankees." In another telling missive written to Vance right after the Burnsville Raid, Robert Blackstock spoke of five different families that chose to relocate. Some went to Asheville, while others headed to McDowell County.[133]

Longstreet received orders from Robert E. Lee to rejoin the Army of Northern Virginia in early April 1864. With regular Confederate soldiers heading to fight in the wilderness, local Unionists and dissidents were emboldened with a new sense of freedom to inflict terror on their neighbors. One newspaper reported continual exchanges between the pickets at Marshall and Kirk's men. It was even reported that local forces abandoned Marshall, retreating to Asheville. The *Charlotte Democrat* advised local citizens to arrest every Tory they could "and make way with him before he has an opportunity to do harm." It was presumed that to "make way with him" referred to sending Tories to the prisons in Asheville or Salisbury. Governor Vance wrote to Confederate secretary of war James Seddon in April, requesting that a regular regiment of Confederate troops be sent to the area. If the population in the western part of the state's only protectors were the local forces, then "starvation must ensue by the wholesale….Time will suffice to tell you of all the horrors to which they are exposed."[134]

While the majority of the veteran Confederate forces had departed East Tennessee, there were clashes between Federals and local Confederate units. On April 24, elements of the Tenth Michigan Cavalry and Third Indiana Cavalry rode toward Jonesborough, charged with the destruction of the bridges and the rails all the way to Carter's Depot, along with attempting to verify Longstreet's rumored departure. Federal cavalry found Confederates in Jonesborough and charged. The Confederates countered but were driven from the town. Federal forces then divided, taking two different paths toward Carter's Depot. At DeVault's Ford, the Federals were able to scatter Confederate defenders, but high water prevented them from fording the Watauga River. At the depot, Confederate pickets were chased back into their works, which were manned by three companies of Thomas's Legion, along with some members of the Fourth Kentucky Cavalry, all under the command of Major William Stringfield. The Federal troopers dismounted and moved to the top of a hill, trading shots with the defenders. Not long thereafter, Stringfield received orders to withdraw to the other side of the bridge. "I obeyed the order under protest knowing that I would be subjected to a galling fire in crossing the bridge," the major later wrote. "As soon as I started from my works, the Yanks commenced yelling & dashed forward to occupy my place." Stringfield quickly ordered his men into position along the western bank of the river and opened a galling fire on the Federals. The troopers retreated to the abandoned Confederate works. Later in the day, Stringfield managed to get his men across the river, and darkness brought a lull in the action.[135]

The morning of April 25 brought a few scattered shots from opposing pickets. Given the strength of the Confederate position on the opposite bank of the river, Federal forces chose not to cross. The Carter's Depot bridge was left intact. Skirmishing ended by mid-morning, and the Federals moved back down the tracks, burning the bridges, with Confederate cavalry following them for a short distance. Confederate losses were placed at one killed, four wounded and five captured. Federal losses were estimated at three killed, twenty-four wounded and six missing or captured.[136]

There were several confrontations in Haywood County as the calendar rolled from April into May. It was reported that two of the three leaders of a recent raiding party, "Jaynes and Jenkins," had been killed. Williams, the other man, had escaped and "threatens that for every man of his killed, five southern men were [to be] shot down in retaliation." A group known as Captain Henry's Scouts was "doing good business in keeping them back and killing many of them." The writer hoped that Colonel Palmer could keep the scouts employed throughout the summer. Henry's Scouts could not be in every place all the time. In early May came reports of a group of dissidents emerging from Laurel to raid farms in the West Fork community. The band was composed of fourteen men and three women. They killed one local citizen, "beat another nearly to death, and then robbed several" others. As the group passed near Mars Hill, they were overtaken, presumably by a local Home Guard command. One of the men and a woman were captured. The newspaper stated that they were all from Buncombe County and that the "women were armed with revolvers and took a hand in the murder and robbery."[137]

Back in Haywood County, at the end of May, another raid was reported. This one deprived locals of their horses. "The people in that section will be unable to make a crop, unless they are protected against the incursions of these Tennessee thieves," a regional newspaper proclaimed. Protecting livestock was a constant struggle. In Sevier County, Thomas Denton hid a pony and milk cow in a cave on English Mountain. The mouth of the cave was covered by fresh brush, and the livestock were let out at night to graze. In neighboring Cocke County, horses were kept in the basement of the Beechwood Hall home. On Upper Jacks Creek, in Yancey County, a Doctor Williams was out plowing his cornfield with his twenty-year-old daughter Emily when some "Union renegades" were spotted coming in their direction. Williams slipped off into the woods, and Emily was left with the horse. "We need that horse," the men told the young lady. Holding the bridle, she said, "It is our only work-horse and you can't have it." "We need it, and we will kill you if we have to," the horse thieves threatened. The workhorse was unhitched from the plow and led away from the family. In Greene County, the women of the Russell family kept their milk cow hidden in a sinkhole near their farm.[138]

Pilfering livestock was not a crime exclusively practiced by the members of one side in the conflict, and the victims were not always those of opposing loyalties. Provost Marshal Samuel P. Carter in Knoxville received complaints from Cocke County. Apparently, the pro-Union Home Guard was "engaged in horse stealing and plundering citizens indiscriminately, Union as well as secession sympathizers." A month earlier, Carter had arrested Major Dunn, the head of the Maryville Home Guard, for a related complaint. In Cocke County, Carter ordered Wade Newman to disband his company. If he refused, then the group would be considered "robbers and outlaws" and treated accordingly. Carter later had to send someone to the area to investigate stolen horses and to arrest Newman if he was involved.[139]

As early as May 1864, the Union high command was considering a raid against the railroad in Western North Carolina. Supplies of all kinds were transported from near Morganton in Burke County toward the east, supplying not only regional Confederate forces but those in Virginia as well. The two large armies in Virginia were battling throughout the spring and

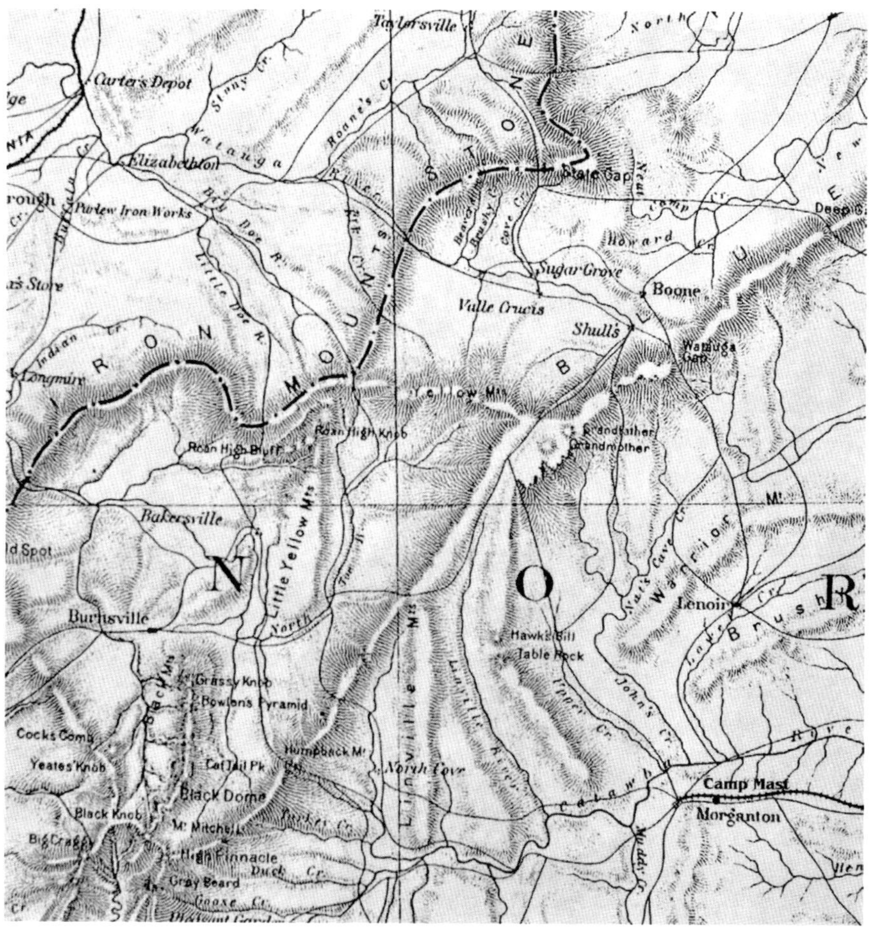

Kirk's force passed over Roan Mountain and across the North Toe and Linville Rivers to reach Camp Vance in June 1864. The camp was just east of Morganton. *Author's collection.*

summer of 1864, and anything that the Federals could do to inflict further damage to the Army of Northern Virginia might advance the success of the Union cause.[140]

Orders were sent from Major General Schofield to Kirk. On June 11, Kirk was officially promoted to captain of Company A, Third North Carolina Mounted Infantry (U.S.). The following day, a portion of the Second North Carolina Mounted Infantry (U.S.), under Lieutenant John Shelton, was detached and ordered to join Kirk. Schofield authorized Kirk, with what men he had already collected, and the detachment under Lieutenant Shelton, to proceed into North Carolina "and destroy the Rail Road between Salisbury and Greensboro...particularly the bridge over the Yadkin River." Kirk was to leave immediately, but he could choose his own route. Kirk's exact plans are generally unknown. In 1912, one possible participant or witness wrote that Kirk planned "to go on to Salisbury....We had an engineer along for the purpose of running the locomotive and a car or two to carry us to Salisbury, where we intended to release the Federal prisoners confined there, arm them, and bring them back with us." Whether this was an official goal of the mission or simply part of the banter among the Unionists as they plodded along is not known.[141]

To accomplish his assignment of destroying the bridge over the Yadkin River near Salisbury, Kirk needed a train. By 1863, the Western North Carolina Railroad had not quite reached Morganton. The terminus of the line was at Speagle's Turnout, about two and a half miles east of the town. At this location, there was a conscript camp known as Camp Vance. When the conscription law was modified to accept men from the ages of forty to forty-five in late summer 1863, Camp Vance opened. New recruits and conscripts, along with captured deserters, were all sent to Camp Vance and then transported east on the railroad. Barracks were built at the new camp, probably named in honor of the governor, along with officers' quarters, a hospital and a guardhouse. At various times during the war, men, often conscripts themselves, served as guards at Camp Vance. Albert Thompson, a member of the local battalion, wrote in August 1863 that they had been out scouting. "[T]ell the folks that our boys has taken the Brest works of the diserters and only fired four guns and took some diserters and shot one mans arm off clost to his shoulder and they shot at too more they never got," he wrote to his wife, Cate.[142]

Later, the Conscription Act was extended to seventeen-year-olds. These young men were ordered to report to various camps in North Carolina to receive training. They were supposed to be assigned to guard details, protecting railroads and warehouses. Eventually, they saw combat action as well. D. Columbus Setzer was one of those recruits. The Caldwell County native was just sixteen years old when he enlisted on May 25, 1864. From Camp Vance, Setzer penned a letter home on June 23:

> *Dear Father, I now Seat myself to inform you that I am well and hearty. the object of my writing this letter is to inform you that we are going to leav her tomorrow morning bright and early fore Raleigh. their we will remain untill further orders. from there we will proceed to Weldon or goldsborough or Kinston. it is uncertain how long we will stay in Raleigh. Sam says we*

> *will stay untill we draw Arms and clothings. the arms we drawed here we returned them today and all our Accourtments....* [W]*e elected a major this morning...Our co., that is co. C, and Co. A and co. B is a going...* [T]*he rest is going to stay.*[143]

Setzer was a part of the Eighth Battalion North Carolina Junior Reserves, and the three companies he mentioned were on their way to Raleigh the following morning.

It is not really possible to know how many of the Second North Carolina Mounted Infantry (U.S.) came with Lieutenant Shelton. Overall, Kirk's force was rumored to include 125 to 130 men. Some were new recruits for Kirk's own Third North Carolina, and some were Cherokee, while others were Confederate deserters. The group set out on foot from Greeneville a couple of days after receiving orders. As they moved through Washington County, word reached the band that Captain Thomas Osborne and his scouts were approaching. Osborne's Scouts were reported in Blount and Sevier Counties in March 1864, shooting and killing several loyalists. One Federal investigation claimed that his men had "set fire to the dwellings of Union men to force them to tell where their money was, to force them to deliver it; failing in this, they have taken them to trees and hanged them." Osborne was apparently returning from delivering prisoners to Bristol on June 19. Kirk concealed his men in a wheat field near Broylesville and, as the scouts were riding down the road, ambushed them. Osborne was mortally wounded, as were several others.[144]

Onward moved Kirk's band. On June 25, in the Crab Orchard section of Carter County, Joseph V. Franklin was recruited as a guide. Using the same route as countless others, Kirk's band crossed over Hump Mountain, moved down Roaring Creek and forded the North Toe River. They halted near the home of David Ellis, a local Unionist, who fed the raiders. On June 26, they crossed the Linville Mountain "about a mile below Pineola," where they camped again and picked up John Franklin as a guide. A long day was in store for June 27. The band pushed down Linville Mountain. Instead of going into camp as darkness settled over the mountains, they pressed on, crossing Upper Creek and taking the Piedmont road. They crossed the Catawba River at Rocky Ford and forded Hunting Creek at the Sudderth Mill. Finding no pickets surrounding Camp Vance, the raiders then stealthily surrounded the camp about daylight. Considerable fog blanketed the area.[145]

Camp Vance commander Major Jesse McLean was absent. The press circulated the story that, on the day before the attack, McLean learned that a group of "300 raiders" had robbed the Tate place. While investigating the matter, McLean came to the conclusion that the group really numbered fewer than twenty and had already fled back over the mountains toward Tennessee. Thus, he felt no apprehension about leaving the camp.[146]

Oran Pine, a Vermont soldier captured during the Battle of Cold Harbor in Virginia, had escaped while being transported through Charlotte. His travels took him close to Camp Vance. Eventually, Pine reached Federal lines, stumbling into Kirk's camp. After hearing of his journey, Kirk invited Pine to join the expedition. Pine recalled surrounding the camp:

> *Cautiously peering over a hill we saw the men assembled for roll call and breakfast. It was arranged that instead of a charge, surrender should be demanded through a flag of truce. Colonel Kirk had a shirt which had once been white. This was torn and the flag attached to two hickory sticks, and a young man, Coburn by name, on detached service from the First Ohio Heavy Artillery, together with myself, approached the guard, who greeted us with "Hello, Yanks! Come to give your colors up?" After stating that we had a message for the post commander we were admitted to headquarters where Lieutenant Bullock was temporarily in command. He had not arisen, but got up from his bunk at our admission, when I saluted and handed him this order: "Commander Camp Vance: You are requested to surrender this camp unconditionally in five minutes. By order of George W. Kirk, Colonel Commanding the Third North Carolina Mounted Infantry U.S." This was a high sounding order for the leader of a hundred men.... Simultaneously with our entrance into headquarters' cabin, a squad of Indians under Captain William Kirk and twenty-five white men under Colonel Kirk encircling the camp...Lieutenant Bullock came out of his room and said "Those Yankee sons-of-guns are all around us. How many men have you?" "Enough to annihilate this camp in ten minutes" I replied. And after being assured that all would receive honorable treatment, the camp was surrendered without firing a gun. The Indians were placed about the camp, the arms...were stacked, and the ammunition thoroughly guarded before the reserve over the hill was brought into camp and our real number disclosed.... The postman and all who approached the camp were taken into custody and arrangements made to prepare rations for our return journey.*[147]

One report stated that there were 240 junior reserves in camp that morning. It is not clear how many other men were present. The young men were in the process of being organized into three companies. They had elected officers the day before but apparently had not been issued muskets for training purposes. At least 8 officers, 2 noncommissioned officers and 121 conscripts or privates were listed as being captured and incarcerated in Northern prison camps. Many others escaped, some in the early morning hours, and others slipped away as the group retreated over the mountains. Sidney F. Conrad was elected a captain in one of the companies on June 27. His records state he was captured; then, in the confusion, some of his friends covered him with a branch as he hid in a ravine. Conrad made his escape soon thereafter. In October, he was elected captain of Company E, First Battalion, North Carolina Junior Reserves. According to one report, another 70 men were saved by the camp surgeon, who managed to get them on the sick list and into the hospital building. If all of the 70 added to the sick rolls were from the junior reserves, that still leaves 39 men.[148]

Kirk sent part of his force toward Morganton, while he led a small group toward the railroad depot. Andrew Murphy, the train conductor, was robbed of his watch and then shot. Before the depot was taken, the telegraph operator is believed to have fired off a message. At the depot, Kirk found a locomotive with three cars and some commissary stores. Here was the train that he needed to complete his mission. It is not clear why Kirk did not continue with his assignment. Blackstock McDaniel, writing on July 7 from Morristown to Governor Johnson, believed that Kirk lacked the men to proceed any further. With the telegraph already alerting those down the line regarding the raid, it would only be a matter of time before the Home Guard and other Confederate forces began converging on his location. Plus, it had already been noted that the Second North Carolina Mounted Infantry (U.S.) lacked discipline. Maybe his men were set on plunder and refused to go further. For whatever reason, Kirk set fire to the depot and cars and damaged the engine.[149]

As a small group of raiders on stolen mounts approached Morganton, they stopped to water their horses in Hunting Creek. Members of the Lowdermilk family had slipped into town and raised the alarm. According to one account, about fifty "furloughed soldiers and the old men above conscript age" formed a line across the road. William W. Avery, a former Confederate congressman and Confederate officer, took charge of the band. Robert C. Pearson and A. Hamilton Erwin rode forward as scouts. Seeing the two approaching, Hackney Norton rode forward, and as the pair came in range, he leveled his rifle in their direction. Pearson supposedly muttered, "May the Lord have mercy on your pour soul" and "loosed a load of buckshot in him and his mule," killing both Norton and his mount. The other members of the party scampered back toward Camp Vance.[150]

Back at the camp, Kirk ordered all of the buildings torched, except the hospital. Once the raiders left the camp, the surgeon and the others were able to save some of the buildings. According to one report filed a few days later, lost were "650 bushels of corn…about 6,500 pounds of forage, some 100 bushels of rye, and 50 of oats; also some 250 guns and accouterments, a goodly number of which were in bad condition, about 1,500 rounds of ammunition….They burned all the office books and papers and all papers and documents in the quartermaster's commissary departments. They took off 4 government mules and 4 private horses, leaving the 2 wagons and 1 set of harness." Oran Pine recalled being sent out into the countryside to tell the "poor people" to come and get whatever provision they could. Local citizens were robbed indiscriminately. One newspaper reported that at least one hundred horses and mules were taken, "forty to fifty negroes carried off"; ladies were robbed of their "valuables, jewelry, spoons…and gentlemen of their money, watches, saddles, &c." The mother of local Unionist R. Tod Caldwell was reportedly robbed of seventeen horses. Another account stated that local people were robbed of "negroes, horses and mules, guns, money, jewelry, silverware, and in some cases clothing." One account in the *Carolina Watchman* mentioned eight people being robbed. Added to the list were three captured free black railroad hands. With Camp Vance in flames, Kirk moved his band back across the Catawba River and went into camp. Pine wrote that they camped at the home of a "very rabid rebel who had some fine hams in his smokehouse." One of the captured junior reserves was seventeen-year-old James Parlier, who later recalled that after the camp was burned, "we were then sent in a north direction, coming to the Catawba river, where 12 of us boys crossed the river in a bateau, all at the same time," around midnight. After spending the night under guard, Parlier and the other boys were placed under the watchful eyes of twenty-eight Indians, "Kirk riding back, giving order to the Indians if any of us boys left the road three steps to shoot us down. (Kirk was looking for State Guards to attack him.) We had not gone very far when the militia began on us. Here old Major Kirk was wounded," and "we all ran away."[151]

Word quickly spread to the surrounding communities about the raid. About 10:00 p.m., a train from Salisbury arrived, containing "one hundred or more citizens and guards." One correspondent believed that this swelled their numbers to "more than three hundred," double what Kirk had. Uncertainty gripped the forces pursuing Kirk. They were unclear which specific route he had taken. Word arrived that the raiders were plundering the countryside beyond the river. Most of the Confederate forces were composed of Home Guardsmen, and thanks to the unwilling and unfortunate farmers the raiders encountered, Kirk's force was now largely mounted. Home Guard forces moved out about 10:00 a.m. on June 29, giving Kirk's men a half-day start. The going was rough. One report stated that many of the soldiers fell out along the route. On at least three different occasions, various forces attempted to stop Kirk's Raiders as they retreated. At one of these skirmishes, near where the Piedmont Springs Road crosses Upper Creek, local forces from Morganton fired a volley into the Federals. Returning fire, Kirk's men killed Phillip Chandler and wounded Doctor Pearson in the knee. In the ensuing mêlée, Kirk placed some of his captives in front of his own men, forcing the unfortunate prisoners to serve as human shields. The drummer boy from Camp Vance was struck and killed, while several others were wounded. Supposedly, Kirk was heard shouting scornfully, "Look at the damned fools, they're shooting their own men!" Later, Home Guard forces attacked again as Federal forces were positioned to the north of Brown Mountain. William W. Avery was leading the assault when he was shot in the groin. Solomon Laws recalled, "After we fired a few rounds the woods were full of smoke. I could see a white object dodging about among the trees, and I kept throwing my eight-shooter on it, as nearly as I could, and firing as it moved from place to place. When the firing ceased and we started to the position of the enemy, a comrade said, 'Laws, you did shoot like hell, and at the crack of your gun I saw a white horse fall.'" Laws believed he had shot Avery, who lingered for a few days before his death. Kirk himself was struck in the arm in one of the skirmishes, the lead ball breaking the bone. One wounded Home Guard member was asked by Kirk how many men were with the local forces. "Five hundred," was the answer. "What in the hell was five hundred attacking three thousand for?" Kirk retorted.[152]

Fog soon enveloped the mountains, and after discarding a large portion of their plunder in the Jonas Ridge area, Kirk and his band managed to escape. After crossing over the mountain once again, Kirk camped for the night near Crossnore. A couple of local men whom Kirk had freed from the stockade at Camp Vance, brothers Doran and Drury Clark, volunteered to go and burn Colonel Palmer's house in the present-day Altamont area. Doran Clark was a deserter from the Fifty-Eighth North Carolina. Palmer's home was considered the finest in the area before falling to the torch of Kirk's new lackeys. It was also rumored that the Chambers house was burned. Over the years, many stories have endured chronicling the depredations committed by Kirk's men through the North Toe River communities and farmsteads. "Kirk's Militia had passed through the country leaving many homes bare," Arizona Hughes recalled many years later. Hughes's mother was forced to return to her parents' house after being robbed. She also recalled that one of her aunts followed the raiders across Yellow Mountain Gap and into Carter County, looking for the stolen horses, which she did find, and that she was actually able to reclaim and return them. However, her exposure to the bad weather brought on pneumonia, and she later died. Kirk entered the home of John Franklin in Pineola, but Franklin did not know he was speaking to Kirk. "If I had some guns, I'd get Jack English and a few other fellows and we'd kill the damn rascal," Franklin exclaimed when he heard of the raid. "Damn you, I am George Kirk," the Unionist stated as he started to draw his pistol. Franklin's wife fell to her knees, shouting, "Lord, don't let him kill John." Franklin quickly replied, "Mr. Kirk, I always knowed you was not half as mean as they said you were." Kirk spared the life of Franklin, who, as the story goes, named his next son "George Kirk Franklin." Several of Kirk's men were wounded, and Kirk sought a doctor in the Spanish Oak Mountain area to extract the ball from his arm. He came across Dr. Axer Pyatt, who performed the operation on Finch Beech. The patient was forced to stay behind at the cabin of Sam English, and it was reported that his family came to visit him, while others brought him provisions. Another wounded man was left at the home of Andrew Buck in Crab Orchard.[153]

William W. Avery served in the North Carolina General Assembly prior to the war. He was appointed to the Confederate Congress and was organizing his own battalion when he was mortally wounded during Kirk's Raid on Camp Vance. *North Carolina Museum of History.*

Just three years after the war, disturbing stories surfaced, describing the treatment some of the prisoners endured at the hands of Kirk and his men. A citizen was passing through some woods at the foot of Paint Mountain in Madison County when he found five piles of sun-bleached bones. He was told by locals that they were the remains of men captured at Camp Vance. These five had escaped and were trying to make their way back to their homes when they were caught by a band of robbers from Laurel or from Greene County. The five were "taken to a secluded spot, and there were all shot dead." The man who discovered the remains was looking for their families and, if no one came forward, was planning on burying them himself. "Four of them were men grown, and one was a very small boy...15 or 16." Another story, even more troubling, emerged in 1870 about the fates of some eight or ten "boys" Kirk had captured. "After getting them into Tennessee, it is said Kirk allowed a few of them to escape. Having stopped on their return to North Carolina to get dinner, these unfortunate boys were overtaken by a detachment of Kirk's men and deliberately marched out from the house and shot! Messrs. Benjamin Inman and Wm Shelt Ray, of Madison county, were present begging for the boys." The two accounts could actually refer to the same event, but other details are lacking.[154]

Kirk's band rode into Knoxville sometime around July 9 to a hero's welcome. He was presented with a uniform, a sword and a sash by local citizens. One newspaper reported that Kirk was "so overcome with emotion that he could but make a brief reply...but all could see that he felt volumes." Other citizens soon stepped forward, speaking on the unjust way Federal soldiers were treated in East Tennessee. One man mentioned that he had been dragged out from his home and forced to sleep for six nights on a hard board. He had not seen his family in eleven months. Horace Maynard rounded out the festivities. Word went up the chain of command, praising the success of the raid. Schofield told Sherman that Kirk brought in 132 prisoners, plus 32 black men and 48 horses and mules, plus an additional 40 men for the Third North Carolina Mounted Infantry (U.S.). Many of the black men, most probably slaves taken from Burke County families, joined the First United States Heavy Artillery (Colored). "Please convey to Col. [*sic*] G.W. Kirk the assurances of my appreciation of the services rendered by him in his late expedition," Sherman wrote back. However, instead of taking on such "hazardous expeditions," Sherman encouraged Kirk to simply work on organizing "the element in North Carolina hostile to Jeff. Davis." Sherman suggested a series of Unionist companies in Western North Carolina that could support one another and provide information on the movements of local Confederates. Kirk's raid on Camp Vance was covered in the newspapers of Philadelphia, New York and Columbus, Ohio.[155]

North Carolina and Confederate forces were left perplexed by the speed of the raid. Colonel Peter Mallett, in charge of the Conscription Bureau in North Carolina, wrote to his commanding officer that Western North Carolina was in an utterly "defenseless condition." Even though

Unionist Horace Maynard represented Tennessee in the U.S. Congress during part of the war. He returned to the House after the war, then served as minister to the Ottoman Empire and as postmaster general. *Library of Congress.*

Camp Vance was not in his district, Palmer communicated the news to his superior in Richmond as well. Palmer had sent some of his meager forces to reinforce Home Guard troops in Mitchell County. Palmer believed that had he been notified earlier, he might have had some troops in a better position to intercept Kirk's band. "I fear this is but the prelude to something more serious," he wrote. Palmer had to keep his limited number of troops posted between Yancey and Cherokee Counties. Some of the recently organized junior reserves had been sent to the eastern part of the state, Palmer complained, and he was in desperate need of cavalry. His only battalion had been disbanded and sent to other regiments on the first of June. Palmer's appeal for more troops this time was even more personal. On Kirk's "return to Tennessee he plundered and burned my residence in Mitchell County," Palmer wrote to Samuel Cooper. "This outrage was committed with a boldness which should stir up our people to vigilance and arm for their own defence…citizens should prepare to protect themselves," one Statesville newspaper editor wrote.[156]

Following on the heels of the capture of the camp, newspapers were rife with rumors of incursions. One Raleigh newspaper reported almost two weeks after the capture of the camp that there were three thousand Federal soldiers in Laurel and another seven hundred in Burnsville. The raid on Camp Vance was just a tiny drop in a vast bucket of military actions during the Civil War. Yet it was the deepest penetration by Unionists into Western North Carolina to date. Kirk was even reported to be raiding as far east as Yadkin County in North Carolina. If Kirk and his band could move so far into the heart of the Confederacy, then Asheville, Statesville or even Charlotte, with all of its Confederate war machinery, including ironworks and a naval yard, were vulnerable to raiding and destruction.[157]

George W. Kirk was now the scourge of many Southerners living in the mountains. Writing from Tennessee, William Gibbs described Kirk as "the notorious robber and murderer…who made up a command from East Tennessee and western North Carolina, and comprised of deserters and the scum of the country generally…men of bad standing and of extremely disreputable characters who, before the war, were regularly before the courts for nearly every species of crime." A family member wrote to Mary Cowles in Wilkes County: "You speak of the Kirk raiders and say again you are not afraid of them—surely you do not believe all the stories that are told of them desperate fellows or you would be frightened to death." The *Charlotte Democrat* considered Kirk a "notorious tory." In reporting the broken arm

Kirk sustained in a skirmish on the retreat, the *Daily Confederate* regretted that it had not been a broken neck.[158]

Kirk's foray into North Carolina was not the only military activity at the time. Famed Confederate cavalry general John H. Morgan was assigned command of the Department of Western Virginia and East Tennessee in late June. His men had been foraging in Washington and Greene Counties. From Nashville, Andrew Johnson took action on his own. Johnson, as military governor, had command of the Governor's Guard, a brigade of cavalry under the command of Alvan C. Gillem. Johnson ordered Gillem to "kill or drive out all maurauders [*sic*]" in East Tennessee and in neighboring states. Gillem was even allowed to attack Morgan's headquarters in Abington. With 1,200 men, Gillem moved from Knoxville through Strawberry Plains, capturing some of Morgan's men. Gillem continued to press on, driving Confederates out of Rogersville, Bull's Gap and Greeneville. Morgan's men fell back to Washington County. It was probably during this time that some of Morgan's men were rumored to have set fire to the homes of 37 Johnson County Unionists, forcing them from the area and possibly killing several other individuals. Daniel Ellis reported that some of Morgan's men were also in Carter County, with orders to burn the Union pilot's house. According to Ellis, local Confederate citizens prevented the soldiers from carrying out these orders.[159]

Skirmishing seemed to happen in almost every county on a daily basis. In Ashe County, Lieutenant Isaac Wilson, a former member of the Thirty-Seventh North Carolina Troops and now a recruiting officer, was bushwhacked in a field as he worked behind his plow. The same thing happened in Madison County. May Holcomb, a member of the Fourteenth Battalion North Carolina Cavalry, was killed and scalped. Ellis recalled a company of Confederates encamped on the Watauga River, "two miles" from his home in Carter County. Ellis, who was prone to hyperbole, embellishment and outright invention, considered this group to be "a most graceless set of villains….They were certainly the worst and most unfeeling set of scoundrels that had ever before been sent into Carter County, and the vile infamy of their conduct towards the Union people will be long remembered by those who had to endure the terrible oppression." In one of those skirmishes, Ellis and some others were sitting on a hill overlooking his house when three "robbers" approached his house. Ellis and two of his comrades were armed with repeating Spencer rifles. Shots were exchanged, and the robbers quickly retreated. Ellis and his two companions hid out in the woods that night and, on returning from a spring early the next

Strawberry Plains was one of the bridges targeted during the 1861 raid. The area served as a depot and a defensive position during the war. *Library of Congress.*

morning, were discovered by a party of "rebels." Ellis had left his Spencer with his friends, and upon spotting him, the rebels "opened a heavy fire." He was able to make it back to his "coveture" and, after he and his comrades concealed themselves, "made good use of our guns." Ellis estimated the attacking party was a mixed force of infantry and cavalry, numbering at least thirty-four. While the two sides battled, a portion of the Rebels plundered Ellis's home. As the robbers retreated, Ellis and the others gave chase. The robbers stopped at a cabin a mile away to get water, and Ellis and one of his companions again opened fire. "One of them was just raising the cup to his lips when a Spencer ball whistled past his ear," Ellis wrote. "[H]e immediately dropped his cup, and all of them started again on a run, and we after them, shooting and yelling in a most terrible manner." The robbers returned to their lair, supposedly sustaining several wounded.[160]

In Western North Carolina, the Sixty-Eighth North Carolina had been transferred from Goldsboro to Morganton. The regiment was charged "with the defence of that section of the Country East of the Blue Ridge… embraced in the Counties of Caldwell, Burke, McDowell, Catawba, Alexander, and Iredell." Regimental commander Colonel James W. Hinton had orders to call on the Home Guard in each of the counties to reinforce his men if needed. In Hinton's orders, the adjutant general painted a picture of the attitudes of many in the western part of the state: "That section of the Country has recently been visited by Raiders from East Tennessee and it is well und[er]stood that another [raid] of a more formidable Character is now being fitted out. As it will be impracticable to guard all the Mountain passes, you will find it necessary to intercept him." If the raiders out of Tennessee were not enough, Hinton had to deal with the deserters as well. They were reported to have "banded together committing all manner of crimes and depredations upon the inhabitants. They must be apprehended or destroyed." The regiment was reportedly headquartered in Morganton by July 27, when companies were sent to Yadkin and Wilkes Counties.[161]

Portions of the Sixty-Eighth North Carolina were in Mitchell County by mid-August 1864. They took part in a raid into Tennessee with elements of the Seventh North Carolina Cavalry. John W. Evans, a member of the Sixty-Eighth, recalled the expedition:

> [P]*reparations were made under marching orders to raid the section of country from which Kirk's army* [had come], *and each comrade being provided with as many rations as he could carry, together with a soldier's other equipment, we moved under the command of our Lieutenant-Colonel E.C. Yellowley, and went along the line most of the way as far as graded, of the Western North Carolina Railroad*[,] *then turned off and crossed the Blue Ridge Mountains via Bakersville…and on into* [that part of] *Tennessee known as the Crab Apple section. We then returned on nearly the same line of march as we went. Nothing was accomplished so far as the writer has any knowledge, further than to make an impression upon the people that it would not be wise on the part of Kirk's army to make another raid.…We did not meet an opposing foe nor were attacked saved one gun shot…fired by the enemy in ambush.* [Because of the glare of] *the campfires…against the thickest forest that ever grew on a mountain side* [the bushwhacker could not be spotted] *and no pursuit could be made. The shot…took effect in the thigh of the camp servant of Lieutenant*

> *W.P. Taylor, who was lying on a log bench by a campfire, but…proved to be of no consequence.*
>
> *The marching over the rocky roads was hard to endure, yet the picturesque mountain scenery, the good water, milk, butter, and honey that we found in great abundance will ever be remembered by the members of the Sixty-eighth Regiment.*[162]

Evans did not remember any losses to the Unionists and dissidents in East Tennessee. A wartime newspaper column recorded events differently or spoke of a different raid. The Seventh North Carolina Cavalry was working with the Sixty-Eighth North Carolina Troops, under Major Charles Roberts. During their action, several groups of dissidents were encountered, with eight or ten killed and "about the same number" captured. The Confederate cavalrymen were able to recover personal property, horses and livestock recently captured by the raiders.[163]

Those who had slipped across the lines to join the Union army and then crept back across to recruit or to visit family were often caught in bad situations. It was reported that Ezekiel Kirkendall was caught in August 1864 inside Confederate lines, in a Federal uniform, with papers that allowed him to be absent from the Second North Carolina Mounted Infantry (U.S.) for the purpose of recruiting new soldiers. Kirkendall was taken to Petersburg, where he was executed in February 1865. William Gentry, of the same regiment, was also caught at home in Madison County. Gentry enlisted in September 1863 and deserted a little over two months later. John Shelton was sent into Madison County to round up those absent without leave, and Gentry said he would go back but, at the appointed time, failed to present himself. Another member of his company stated after the war that Gentry made a camp away from his house, so he would not be found. He was discovered by a "Rebel scout," killed and his body thrown "across the fire."[164]

There was also a steady stream of escaped Union prisoners of war moving through the mountains, attempting to reach the Federal lines in East Tennessee. Francis Hosmer, of the Fourth Vermont Infantry, was captured in Virginia on June 23, 1864, during the Battle of Reams Station. While on a train heading south out of Lynchburg, Hosmer and another soldier, Corporal H.T. Gorham, jumped off the train and started west through the Piedmont of North Carolina, eventually reaching Watauga County. The pair ran into a larger group, which Hosmer estimated at a little over 132 men, about half Confederate deserters and the other half dissidents. Their guide, learning that the party had been spotted by two women out picking blackberries,

Escaped prisoners and dissidents trying to make their way across the mountains to Union lines often sought friendly places to stay. One such place was the Old English Inn in Mitchell County. *Author's collection.*

abandoned the group and continued unencumbered to East Tennessee. The group was discovered by "Uncle Billy Cook," a "man of sandy complexion, full beard, about five feet five inches high, probably fifty-five years of age, of pronounced theological views, and a Union man, who had proclaimed his loyalty from the first, and declared that if the Confederacy compelled him to fight he proposed to commence on his own premises. So far he had been watched, but not molested." Uncle Billy brought food and relocated the group to a laurel thicket in the Story settlement. More food was brought by other residents, but feeding such a large group was a burden. Since the mountains were full of local troops looking for this group, Cook advised them to split up "into small parties and make your way the best you can. Some of you can get through in that way, and some will likely be caught." Hosmer and Gorham eventually ran into the Home Guard and were recaptured. They were imprisoned in "an old building," possibly at Camp Mast, with their ally, Uncle Billy Cook, who had been captured separately. The group denied that they had ever met Cook before and probably saved his life. "The next day under a strong guard," recorded Hosmer, "we were marched over the mountain to the little hamlet of Boone, and there quartered in the county jail, an old log building, of two stories, and four rooms." Confined upstairs were the Story sisters, Bettie and Lucy, who had frequently helped Union soldiers. Hosmer believed that they were apprehended about the same time as Cook. Hosmer and Gorham were taken the next day to Camp Vance and then to Salisbury.[165]

Just as they struggled to evade capture by opposing forces, men also went to considerable lengths to stay out of the army altogether. When Confederate soldiers were searching for the Heatherly gang in Carter County, they found a pit beneath a stable. Within the pit were four "unearthly, haggard, bleached" men. When asked about how long they had been in the hole, "About three months" was the reply. The hole was "four feet wide" and "long enough for a man to lie down in; and was shelved on both sides and…an old box in the center, here four men, had been playing cards; by the light of a tallow candle, the shelves were filled with bacon, flour, honey, apple butter, butter, tobacco, clothes, and about a half bushel of chicken bones." Nearby, Confederate soldiers found a basket swinging

Camp Mast, the Home Guard basc in Watauga County, was located on Cove Creek, behind the houses in the center of this photo. *Author's collection.*

in the trees. Fresh loaves of bread and cooked chickens were found inside, and bee gums were discovered close by. In neighboring Watauga County, John Walker, a member of the local Home Guard, decided that he did not want to serve anymore. Nor was he willing to cross over the mountains, losing his social status in the community. Instead, Walker devised a plan in which he was "captured" by six women and two men, all dressed as Federal soldiers. One evening, the "Federal" soldiers marched into Walker's front yard, stopping at the front door and "rapping for admittance. John and his women folk, with white faces, appeared and opened the door." The soldiers demanded Walker's surrender. "There was a parley, John's women pleading for him, with tear-bedimmed eyes." The soldiers had to tear Walker "away from the arms of his family." Word soon spread that there were Yankees in the area, and "France and Wilts Beech…started on horses" to alert the Home Guard. Walker was "taken to a ridge and rock cliff just above" a mill and was "fed by Elisha [Coffey] whenever he went out to feed his hogs. It was about one week later that John walked into his home, apparently much crippled up and sorely distraught, but bearing an iron-clad paper-writing with his signature attached, a duplicate of the one he declared the Yankees in Tennessee had compelled him to sign while in captivity." Walker's ruse worked, and he was not required to perform duty with the Home Guard, at least not for some time.[166]

Various groups continued to spar in East Tennessee. The Thirteenth Tennessee Cavalry (U.S.) left Camp Nelson in late January 1864, moving to Nashville. They were a part of Andrew Johnson's Governor's Guard. For the next few months, new recruits continued to join the regiment, while scouting expeditions commenced in order to obliterate guerrilla bands from the region. Upon the regiment's arrival in Gallatin, Tennessee, a local resident believed the East Tennesseans to be "the meanest men I ever saw." When East Tennessee residents petitioned Johnston in late May 1864 for relief, it was the Thirteenth, along with two other Federal cavalry regiments sent with Gillem, who were assigned to root out the Confederates and secure the foodstuffs. The Thirteenth Tennessee left Nashville on August 1 and arrived in Knoxville on August 17. The men spent the next few days skirmishing in the Rogersville and Morristown areas. Many were anxious to return to the counties along the border, yet the Federals were between Morgan's command to the east and Joe Wheeler's Confederate cavalry to the west.[167]

John Hunt Morgan was planning a raid. He wanted to take Greeneville, then Bull's Gap, before moving on toward Knoxville. His cavalry force set off from Abington on the morning of September 3, with somewhere between 1,800 and 2,000 troopers. Morgan dispatched some men on to Blue Springs, while he set up his headquarters in Greeneville at the Williams home. One Greeneville woman recalled that Morgan's men "pilferd and stoled all they could and bused the wifes and darts [daughters] of union men on miny ways that would not be proper for me to state here for more than one resone." A teenage boy was captured by some of his scouts but later escaped and went straight to the Federal camp at Bull's Gap. After some persuasive negotiations with Gillem, Colonel John Miller was allowed to take the Tennessee regiments to Greeneville. Two columns moved through the darkness. Heavy rain undoubtedly masked their progress. As day broke on September 4, a portion of the Thirteenth Tennessee staged on a nearby hill, waiting for the other columns to move into position. A local citizen warned the commander that Morgan and five thousand Confederate cavalrymen were in town. On learning of Morgan's headquarters at the Williams home, two companies were ordered into action, with orders to take Morgan "dead or alive." Federal cavalry converged on Greeneville, scattering Confederate pickets. Morgan, hearing the commotion, ran outside. Some believe Morgan was killed while attempting to surrender. Others write that he was shot in the back attempting to flee. Regardless, Morgan lay dead in the backyard of the Williams home, killed by Andrew Campbell, a private from the Thirteenth Tennessee Cavalry. Morgan's remains were thrown across a horse and taken outside town. The Confederate cavalrymen were driven from the area, eventually making their way back to Jonesborough. That evening, Gillem ordered the body of Morgan returned to the Williams house. His remains were taken to Abington for burial and then later removed to Lexington, Kentucky. A week after Morgan's death, Confederate and Federal officials met in Greeneville, discussing the exchange of prisoners. It was a fruitless meeting.[168]

Gillem's job was to clear Confederates from East Tennessee. Arriving to take the place of Morgan was John C. Vaughn and his brigade of Confederate cavalry. Vaughn's job was to clear the area of Union soldiers and sympathizers. "No people in the Confederacy has suffered as our relations and friends [in East Tennessee] have," Vaughn wrote. "They are all robbed and imprisoned—not allowed the liberties of Negroes." Filling in as department commander was Brigadier General John Echols. In a letter to Richmond, Echols agreed with Vaughn's appraisal of the situation: "The condition of East Tennessee is a very bad one, the large majority of the people being opposed in sentiment to us, and the country being filled

John Hunt Morgan's cavalry command raided as far north as Ohio. Morgan was killed in Greeneville in September 1863. *Library of Congress.*

with bushwhackers and marauders in organized bands. Murders are almost daily occurrence on the persons of peaceable citizens, and enormities and atrocities are constantly being perpetrated."[169]

On September 20, Kirk was promoted to lieutenant colonel of the Third North Carolina Mounted Infantry (U.S.). By September 20, at least on paper, the Third North Carolina had 445 men on the roster. It is interesting to note that Kirk's command was not a part of the Governor's Guard. Instead, they were members of the Second Brigade, Fourth Division, XXIII Corps. Brigadier General David Tillson was their brigade commander and Jacob Ammen their division commander.[170]

War in the counties along the borders was being waged relentlessly. The Reverend Robert B. McCall, sometimes chaplain of the Thirteenth Tennessee Cavalry (U.S.) and other times a Federal scout, was working his way through the lines with "a large company of Union men." They had stopped at Seaton's Mill on Middle Creek in Greene County when guerrillas surprised them and captured McCall; William Davis, a recruiting officer; and Richard Allen, a "lieutenant" in an unknown regiment. McCall had field glasses on his person. He was accused of being a spy and "was immediately shot." Davis had recruiting papers on him and was bayoneted. Allen was taken into a nearby cedar thicket, stripped of his clothing and shot in the head. According to a later history, Allen "had picked the bullet out of the wound with his own fingers." He was found and taken to a nearby home, where he died eleven days later.[171]

Gillem's and Vaughn's commands continued to clash through the fall. Vaughn surprised the Federals on September 22 at Bull's Gap, preventing Gillem's and Jacob Ammen's brigade from participating in the raid in Virginia. Vaughn slowly pulled back, and his 600 troopers thwarted the efforts of nearly 2,500 Federals. After the first Battle of Saltville failed, Gillem and Ammen returned to Greeneville. Vaughn attacked on October 12, and the Federals fell back to Bull's Gap. Three days later, Confederate cavalry burned the bridge over Mossy Creek and tore up two miles of track, cutting off the Federals at Bull's Gap from their supply base at Knoxville. Gillem and Ammen were again forced to retreat. John C. Breckinridge, now in command of the district, telegraphed Vaughn: "I am much gratified at your recent success, and General Lee has also expressed his satisfaction." There were skirmishes on October 16 and 18, both Confederate victories.[172]

Writing from his headquarters in Rheatown, Vaughn issued the following proclamation:

> *Notice is hereby given to all bushwhackers, outlaws and deserters in the counties of Carter, Johnson, Greene, Washington, &c, that any more acts of robbing, or killing or wounding of any Confederate soldiers or citizens, committed by them, will subject the houses and property of them and their friends in the vicinity of the place where the crime is committed, to be burnt to the ground.*[173]

Back in North Carolina, John B. Palmer received orders from General Lee to coordinate with Breckinridge's and Vaughn's forces. It appears that he had made a short foray into Cocke County in late September or early October. His presence added pressure to Gillem's and Ammen's commands, contributing to their retreat. When this new directive came, Palmer consolidated his forces in Madison County and, on October 19, moved eight hundred men and three cannons through Cocke County and toward Mossy Creek. Palmer claimed that it was his men who had burned the bridge. Palmer met with Vaughn on the twenty-first and then took his force on to Russellville, destroying the railroad and gathering telegraph wire, returning to Bull's Gap that evening. On October 27, Palmer was ordered to have his men ready to move back to Russellville. Vaughn and Gillem clashed outside Morristown on October 28. Overwhelmed by superior numbers, Vaughn was pushed back to the east, eventually falling back as far as Carter's Depot on the Watauga River. Palmer's command covered most of the retreat, eventually breaking off and returning to North Carolina. Palmer reported that he had lost one cannon, a mountain howitzer loaned to Vaughn's command, but that he had been able to bring back "some cattle and hogs, my train loaded with wheat and commissary stores, and some captured horses, mules, and entrenching tools." He also reported that he had captured sixteen men belonging to the Tenth Michigan Cavalry, sent to shadow his troops. Palmer wrote his report from Asheville, dating it November 3, 1864.[174]

Breckinridge pulled forces out of Southwest Virginia and reinforced Vaughn's command. On November 10, Confederate forces were back in Greeneville and drove the Federals into their Bull's Gap entrenchments the next evening. Several times, Breckinridge tried to take the Federal works on November 12, but he failed each time. Palmer rejoined Breckinridge with six hundred North Carolinians the next day, and Breckinridge found an unguarded gap two miles away. That evening, Breckinridge attacked Gillem, who was in the process of retreating. Confederate forces chased Federal troops for twenty-five miles, capturing more than three hundred prisoners, all of Gillem's artillery and most of the Federal ambulances and supply wagons, along with five to six hundred cattle and horses. Federal forces limped back into the Knoxville defenses. For the moment, upper East Tennessee was free from Federal soldiers.[175]

While the larger, more traditional battles between the Blue and the Gray were being waged in East Tennessee, the guerrilla war accelerated. In the Shelton Laurel community, riders rode up to the Granny Franklin cabin. Franklin was a widow, and her four sons had stayed out of the war. As the raiders were spotted, Granny Franklin called out for her boys to grab their rifles. "If you've got to die, die like a damned dog with your teeth in a throat," she later testified telling her sons. Robert, James and Josiah, the three who were home, were between fifteen and nineteen years old. James rushed out on the porch, supposedly shooting one member of the group who was still mounted. As James made for a split-rail fence, he was struck. Robert stepped onto the porch and was also killed. Josiah dove through a window and crawled under the house. A raider tried to crawl in after him, but he was shot. A second raider tried to retrieve his comrade's body, but he was also killed. The remaining raiders decided to set fire to the cabin. Granny Franklin ran outside, only to have a raider fire at her, clipping a piece of her hair. As the smoke began to suffocate Josiah, he crawled out from under the cabin, and his skull was promptly bashed in by the raiders. Granny Franklin survived, but her three sons and several of the raiders did not. History cannot agree on the identity of the raiders. One story maintains that the Franklins were Unionists and that the raiders were some of Colonel James Keith's men. Another story claims the Franklins were pro-Confederate in their sympathies and that the raiding party was led by none other than George W. Kirk himself. There are some who claim that nothing about this story is, in fact, true.[176]

On the heels of this raid came one in Mitchell County with more clearly defined motivations. Between seventy-five and eighty Tories rode into the wilds of the Toe River Valley. They captured twenty-five members of the Home Guard, along with former Confederate officer and state representative Jacob Bowman and county register Robert Lewis. They hit the Robert Young farm, then moved to the Whitson farm. There, they seized the family's pigs and oxen. Samuel McInturff rode up while the raiders were still on site, and "he was shot off the horse" he was riding, one of two men killed that September day. While Kirk was not mentioned in the newspapers at the time, local folklore blamed the Tennessean for the incident.[177]

As fall tightened its grip on the mountains, it was unsafe to be outdoors, even on one's farm. In Johnson County, David Slimp had slipped away in June 1864. When the Federals retook East Tennessee, he thought it safe to visit his family. Robbers burst into the house, demanding money. His wife had actually tossed his pocketbook behind the bed. The vandals then beat Slimp with their pistols, "inflicting dangerous wounds." Slimp survived but complained of his injuries for the rest of his life. Eight "old and infirm men" in Johnson County drafted a resolution to Breckinridge. They complained of "four or five bands of robbers and bushwhackers, who are obstructing the public road, robbing Southern men, and killing them and further threatening to drive us all from the county" and wanted protecting, stating that they were willing to sell their surplus foodstuffs to the government. Robert Blackstock complained to Governor Vance in mid-October that over three thousand Confederate cavalry were in Buncombe County. They were plundering the countryside, taking corn and oats, burning fences and shooting livestock. In late October, two members of Keith's command were bushwhacked and killed as they visited family in Madison County. In Mitchell County, Jackson Stewart, a former Confederate officer and sheriff, was bushwhacked and killed on November 17, 1864. According to local stories, Stewart was appointed tax collector and had seized several horses belonging to local Unionists near Bakersville. They caught up with him, and Stewart was shot eight times. In one account, the Unionists cut off his head and placed it on a pole before riding back into Bakersville.[178]

There were just too few men to guard the passes and to deal with localized bands on the North Carolina side. On December 18, Palmer was reported as having a mere 1,275 men present for duty. Assistant Adjutant General David Urquhart was conducting a tour of the area for Samuel Cooper. Urquhart provided a unique glimpse into Western North Carolina as winter's grip fell upon the area:

> *I have just returned from the Western District of North Carolina. I regret to report a bad state of affairs prevailing there. The country is full of deserters and tories, who are growing bolder every day and committing great outrages, defying the Government and openly avowing that they are acting under orders from the enemy. If active measures are not adopted before the leaves come out, it will be impossible to disperse and capture them. The troops in Colonel Palmer's command are all North Carolinians. He has part of* [the] *Sixty-second and Sixty-fourth Regiments North Carolina Volunteers, who are really deserters and stragglers, as they were absent when these regiments were captured at Cumberland Gap. They will not answer to hunt down these deserters and tories. I recommend that a Virginia regiment be sent up there as soon as it can be spared to clear the mountains near the North Carolina line….All the deserters are harbored by the natives, especially by the women. A rigid system of police should be established and the house of all these harborers of deserters burnt down….Colonel Palmer understands the nature of the country, and if the department would call him to Richmond and hear his views I feel confident his suggestions would be valuable.*[179]

Colonel Palmer was not the only central figure in the region's drama whose name was known farther afield. George Stoneman had a dubious reputation. A West Point graduate, he had led Federal cavalry south during the Battle of Chancellorsville in May 1863 but had failed to do any tangible damage. After a stint at a desk job in Washington, D.C., he took command of the cavalry of the Department of Ohio, fighting with Sherman in the Atlanta Campaign. Stoneman was captured on July 31, 1864, outside Macon, Georgia. He was the highest-ranking Federal officer captured during the war and was imprisoned for three months. Following his release, Schofield appointed Stoneman his second-in-command of the Department of Ohio. Secretary of War Edwin Stanton wrote to Grant disapproving of Stoneman's appointment: "If you approve of his doing so, I am content, although I think him one of the most worthless officers in service, and who has failed in everything entrusted to him." Stoneman wanted to redeem his reputation. A sudden strike on the salt works in Virginia could deprive Lee's army, along with a large portion of the population in surrounding states, of the vital component necessary for food preservation. Plus, if Stoneman could neutralize the Confederate forces in the area, then North Carolina, and perhaps upstate South Carolina as well, could be open to invasion. There was even a possibility that Salisbury, with its prison and factories, could be taken. Schofield allowed Stoneman to proceed to Saltville but deferred the raid into North Carolina, "until affairs here take a definite shape."[180]

On December 10, 1864, Stoneman launched his raid into Southwestern Virginia. To protect his rear, he ordered the Fourth Tennessee Infantry (U.S.) and Kirk's Third North Carolina Mounted Infantry (U.S.) to hold the mountain passes on the North Carolina–Tennessee border. Palmer had orders to work with Vaughn and to attack Stoneman's rear. On December 20, with elements of the Sixty-Second and Sixty-Fourth, Palmer embarked toward Tennessee, while about two hundred members of Thomas's Legion moved toward Yancey County in an attempt to cut off Kirk's force. A part of the Federal force had advanced as far as Marshall in Madison County. "Every house…was robbed except two," came the report from Marshall. One house was used as the Federal headquarters. The other was protected by an armed lady standing in the doorway, daring the raiders to enter. In another home, raiders destroyed what they could not take. "They emptied… beds and stirred them with molasses and lampblack." It was a cold night by a fire for those still left in the Madison County seat. Palmer considered the Federals at Paint Rock a "formidable force of the enemy," and he found it necessary to "dispose of that force before leaving." It is unclear if the Federals retreated of their own accord or if the two sides skirmished. Palmer then moved into Tennessee. "An unexpected and severe storm so raised the streams" that Palmer was unable to catch up to Stoneman's rear. Instead, he turned his attention to Kirk, who had retreated to Greasy Cove in Washington (now Unicoi) County. Palmer believed that Kirk was going to move against the bridges over the Watauga or Holston Rivers.[181]

While records are vague, Palmer appears to have attempted to surround Kirk at Greasy Cove. Stringfield had the left, while Love's Battalion of Thomas's Legion took the right and Palmer advanced in the center. Before Palmer's forces could converge, Kirk attacked first. On the morning of December 29, 1864, Kirk's men began to move in. Federal soldiers embarked from the vicinity of present-day Unicoi. They were ferried across the Nolichucky River by Marcella Ray and Hannah Edwards, two teenaged locals. Family lore has it that Hannah's red hair came undone and could be seen whipping in the wind as she helped soldiers over the river. Kirk possibly had his men in three different positions, including posted along the line of retreat. James A. Keith, who led some type of band after his resignation from the Sixty-Fourth North Carolina, might have been in the area during the attack. It is rumored that Keith had already burned the home of deserter and Federal guide Hezekiah Horn and then killed Horn. Keith was staying at the home of another Unionist when a rider informed Keith of the attack near the river. Keith and several of his men started in the direction of the sound of the gunfire and clashed with some of Kirk's men near the present-day Shallowford Church. Reportedly, three of the Confederates were killed and buried nearby. Kirk's brother William was wounded in the skirmish. George W. Kirk saw a Confederate soldier about to finish off William and struck the man with his sword, possibly cutting off his head. Confederate soldiers were soon on their way back to Madison County. Palmer made little mention of the skirmish in his report. He only stated that a portion of his command returned to North Carolina without permission and that a large number of his men were "badly shod." Thomas Davis, a member of the Sixty-Fourth North Carolina, wrote home on January 3 that they had covered fifty-six miles in two days but that his detachment was not involved in the fight. It was very cold, Davis wrote, and several of his comrades were barefoot: "[T]he snow and ice cut their feet and the blood run freely." Losses on either side are unknown. Kirk claimed that he "killed 100 of Palmer's men and guerrillas, and wounding a large number, he captured 32 prisoners and 56 horses." There were several of Kirk's men killed or wounded: Gaston Higgins and David Shelton were wounded on December 20; George Doby and John Di-A were killed at Paint Gap on December 23; and on December 24, at Indian Creek in Tennessee, Rufus Laws was killed, William Kirk and James B. Laws were wounded and Andrew and James Laws were captured.[182]

Palmer moved his small command toward Strawberry Plains. He left the Sixty-Second and Sixty-Fourth Regiments to guard Big Creek Gap while he returned to Asheville. Vaughn's cavalrymen were also in the area, but once they fell back, the two North Carolina regiments also departed. They were back in Warm Springs by the time Palmer wrote his report on January 12, 1865. Stoneman's overall Virginia campaign was a success. Federal cavalry destroyed the lead mines in Wythville and the salt works in Saltville.[183]

Across the chessboard of war, the South had suffered numerous defeats in 1864. Lee had been able to fight Grant to a standstill to the north of Richmond, but Grant shifted his armies below the James River to Petersburg and locked the Army of Northern Virginia into a siege. Sherman had taken Atlanta from the Confederates and, by December, had marched his Federal army all the way to Savannah. The Confederate Army of Tennessee had moved north of Atlanta, through Alabama and Tennessee but was wrecked in a series of battles fought at Franklin and south of Nashville. The war was still very real along the Western North Carolina–East Tennessee border. Larger, more conventional actions were taking place on the Tennessee side, while the seemingly endless raids by Federals and guerrilla bands were ripping apart Tar Heel communities. Many were just praying for an end.

5

1865

"Depredations of Guerrillas, Bushwhackers and Similar Assassins"

While there were still skirmishes through the border counties in East Tennessee, much of the action shifted to Western North Carolina as December 1864 shifted to January 1865. In Watauga and Caldwell Counties, the brunt of the war was being waged between the Eleventh Battalion North Carolina Home Guard, under the command of Major Harvey Bingham, and William McKesson Blalock, Malinda Blalock and their band of outlaws.

Bingham started the war as a twenty-three-year-old sergeant in Company E, Thirty-Seventh North Carolina Troops. In December of that year, he was promoted to third lieutenant. During the Battle of Second Manassas in August 1862, Bingham was wounded in the head. He survived but resigned by reason of "disease of the lungs" and returned home to Watauga County. Governor Vance selected Bingham to head the local Home Guard company in 1863, and by 1865, he had two companies under his command. Camp Mast, their headquarters, was located on Cove Creek in the western part of the county. One Federal soldier, captured while attempting to pass through the mountains to the Union lines in East Tennessee, was taken to Camp Mast and described the facility as having "but one street and a row of cabins on either side. There were but fifteen cabins in all, twelve of which were for the privates, one for the officers, and two for horses." According to oral history, the camp was located in a hollow, an attempt to protect the soldiers when the winter winds howled. Bingham's men had done a fair job chasing deserters and battling dissidents. He was even voted a resolution of thanks by the North Carolina General Assembly for his zeal in pursuing the rebellious. However, that success had come at a cost. In the fall of 1864, a group from Carter County had crept into Watauga County. They shot James Farthing and proceeded to the home of Reuben Farthing, stealing several horses. With eighteen of his men, Bingham set out in pursuit. They recaptured some of the livestock, possibly in the Poga area of Carter County, and then captured Bill Gwyn, a Federal soldier who had deserted from the Eighth Tennessee Cavalry (U.S.) earlier that year. The next day, Bingham was ambushed by Union guide James Hartley on the lower reaches of Beech Mountain. The "battle raged all over the timbered knob," it was later reported. Among the mortally wounded was Elliott Bingham, Harvey's younger brother. One Raleigh newspaper reported, "There was quite a severe fight…in Watauga county between a party of deserters, under one Jim Hartley, and a detachment of Home Guards, under Major Bingham. Four of the Home Guard wounded, one mortally. Eight deserters reported killed and several wounded." Later, historians recorded that none of Hartley's group was actually wounded or killed.[184]

William M. "Keith" Blalock and his wife, Malinda Pritchard, lived in Coffey's Gap, near Blowing Rock in Watauga County. With all of the talk of looming conscription in early 1862, Blalock chose to voluntarily enlist in the Confederate army, joining Company F, Twenty-Sixth North Carolina Troops, on March 20, 1862. Samuel Blalock, reportedly Keith's younger brother, also enlisted that day. Samuel was really his wife, Malinda. She had cut her hair and donned men's clothing, disguising her gender to be near her husband. Whether Keith was a part of this ruse from the outset is unknown. Regardless, both were mustered into the Confederate army. The Twenty-Sixth North Carolina was stationed near Kinston during this time. According to her service record, Malinda's "disguise was never penetrated. She drilled and did the duties of a soldier as any other member of the company, and was very adept at learning the manual and drill." As reported in a postwar account, she "wore a private's uniform and tented and messed with Keith. She watched the men 'when they went in swimming'…but never went in herself." One early historian wrote that "Keith was a Union man and joined only to avoid conscription and in the hope that opportunity might offer for him to desert to the Union lines." Deciding after a month that he had endured enough of army life, Keith went into the swamp and rubbed down with poison sumac. He presented himself to the regimental surgeon and was discharged on April 20, 1862, by reason of "hernia" and "poison from sumac." Not wishing to remain in the army on her own, Malinda revealed

James Hartley was a guide and lieutenant in the Third North Carolina Mounted Infantry (U.S.). *Courtesy of Sandra Pierson.*

her secret to her captain, who then took her to the colonel, Zebulon B. Vance. Malinda was discharged, and the couple returned to the mountains. The accounts of the Blalocks and their peculiar military service leave many questions. If Blalock was truly a Union man, then he could have crossed over the mountain like the Banners did and joined the Union army. Or, upon arriving at Kinston, he could have found the Union army, fewer than forty miles distant. Instead of actually being a serious "Union man," Blalock was a dissident. He did not officially join the Union army until mid-1864 and, even then, never left the area. According to his pension record, his officers questioned many of his actions, even going so far as to state that Blalock might have been a deserter from the Union army at times.[185]

The Blalocks carried on their own personal war while the bigger conflict raged. In 1864, Keith Blalock and his band captured William Coffey in Caldwell County. William and his brother Reuben Coffey, step-uncles of Blalock, were "pronounced Southern men" and had zealously sought out men who legally should have been in the Confederate army. Blalock's discharge papers meant little to them, and when he started piloting men through the lines to the Union army, there was open hostility, not only with his step-uncles but with other Confederate conscription officers as well. William Coffey was later caught out plowing his field. The Blalock band took him to James Gragg's mill, where a man named Perkins killed him.[186]

Blalock claimed in his pension application that Bingham captured him and that he was imprisoned in Watauga County for eight days. On his way down the mountain, he managed to escape. In August 1864, the Home Guard, presumably Bingham's men, ambushed Blalock near his Watauga County home. Blalock was wounded in the left arm, and he and Malinda were forced to flee up into the boulder field on Grandfather Mountain. It was later recorded that they were reduced to taking "refuge with some hogs which had 'bedded up' under the rocks." Malinda sent word to the Unionists in Banner Elk, and several of them found the couple and escorted them to the Crab Orchard section of Carter County. Blalock was out of action for a couple of months. He blamed Robert Green of Caldwell County for wounding him. Blalock later caught Green on the road between Blowing Rock and the Globe and shot and wounded him.[187]

In most cases, the war was being fought on a very personal level. Not far from where the Blalocks lived near Blowing Rock, James Carroll was out actively recruiting men for the Federal army. He recalled in 1886 that he and George W. Perkins were "at the house of William Triplett trying to recruit him; that while on their way from Triplett's house to the widow Carroll's… they came upon a party of rebels, being part of the Watauga Home Guard, commanded by Lieut. Lewis Bryant; that said rebels fired upon them, wounding [Carroll] in the right side and hip." One ball entered the right breast of Carroll, breaking one rib and damaging his lung before exiting out his back. The second ball struck Carroll in the thigh, "causing paralysis of the whole leg." John Elrod, a member of the Home Guard, recalled that

William M. Blalock and his wife, Malinda, raided farms in Caldwell and Watauga Counties, while piloting dissidents through the area and toward Tennessee. *Avery County Historical Museum.*

several shots were fired at Perkins and Carroll. Perkins supposedly escaped, while Elrod carried Carroll to his mother's house, the widow Carroll to whose house he and Perkins had been traveling, and dressed his wounds before leaving.[188]

At the same time, Keith Blalock claimed to be nearby, at the home of Madison Estes on the John's River. With several others, he decided to raid the farm of Carroll Moore in Caldwell County. According to one of Blalock's neighbors, the purpose of the raid was to "plunder and steal stock." On January 6, Blalock and a dozen others surrounded the Moore home. In the ensuing shootout, Blalock was shot in the head, the ball destroying one of his eyes. His gang fell back, returning to the Estes home, and eventually made their way back to Carter County. Blalock would survive his wound.[189]

The war was not confined to just Watauga and Caldwell Counties. On January 21, General William T. Sherman issued directives to departmental commander George Thomas. Sherman wanted Thomas to put together a small cavalry force, "say, 2,000 men to operate from Knoxville through the mountains pass along the French Broad into North Carolina, to keep up the belief that it is to be followed by a considerable force of infantry." Sherman was convinced that Stoneman was the man for the job, while Gillem watched the Holston River area. Kirk already had men in the area, recruiting and looking for the enemy. A detachment of the Third North Carolina (U.S.) was sent to Indian Creek to watch for local Confederate activity, in mid-January. The group was attacked, and William Norton was mortally wounded, dying on January 12, 1865. Four days later, Milton Henson was killed by Confederates near Mars Hill College. Henson was reported as being absent from his command, with leave, at the time of his death. Major Stringfield wrote of a raid that same month by an Indiana cavalry regiment near Bryson City in Swain County. Portions of Thomas's Legion "followed and harassed them greatly."[190]

A more significant raid occurred on the first of February 1865. On February 4, Kirk slipped with a sizeable force into Waynesville, in Haywood County. A quick skirmish overwhelmed the Home Guard. They released prisoners being held in the county jail and then burned the building. Other local homes were plundered, and the home of Lieutenant Colonel James Love was burned. "Every horse within reach was taken, and the wardrobes of every lady were most shamefully plundered," it was noted a couple of weeks later. Some accounts have Kirk's men then moving southwest, toward Balsam Gap. But they were attacked that night by local troops, some one hundred local Haywood County farmers. Kirk retraced his steps to Waynesville and then moved toward Soco Gap, where he encountered other troops. Kirk then returned and passed through Balsam Gap. Another account written in February 1865 states that Kirk encountered some of Thomas's Legion at Soco Gap on February 6. The "little band of brave soldiers" had "fought with considerable determination…near the Indian church on Soco creek." Eventually, they were forced to yield, and Kirk's command "passed on without being further molested."[191]

Stories of the atrocities committed by Kirk's men were passed down to family members through the generations. On Jonathan's Creek in Haywood County, Kirk's men shot and killed Absolom B. Carver and James E. Rice, both former Confederate soldiers. They burned the home of Young Bennett in Cataloochee and then burned a school that was serving as a makeshift hospital for sick and wounded Confederate soldiers. It was rumored that Kirk's men executed several of the soldiers before setting the log structure ablaze. When the raiders arrived at the farm of local Unionist Macinda Adele Battle, they found no livestock. A local family had sent a horse, two mules and several cattle into the woods with a slave. Later, one of the raiders returned, and when he tried to take the horse, Macinda shot and killed him, burying him under the dirt floor of the barn, believing that the tramp of the horse would hide the grave. Levi Caldwell and his son Hiram were caught and tied to the front porch of their house while the raiders went into the house to play cards. The Caldwells worked their ropes lose, and when the raiders came back outside to fire the house, the Caldwells ran. Hiram escaped, but Levi was captured, imprisoned and later released. His death not long after the war was attributed to the mistreatment he received at the time of his incarceration.[192]

Word of Kirk's raid spread across the mountains. Home Guard companies were ordered to Morganton in Burke County. There were rumors of up to three hundred local dissidents organizing themselves at Piedmont Springs in northern Burke County. Lieutenant Colonel J.M. Neal of the McDowell County Home Guard was reportedly captured on Muddy Creek between Marion and Morganton by an unknown raider band, and a "gang of desperadoes" ransacked the home of former McDowell County sheriff Mills Higgins. In Asheville, there were attempts to organize the Sixty-Ninth North Carolina Troops, also known as the Seventh North Carolina Cavalry. Portions of the Fourteenth Battalion North Carolina Cavalry were organized in December 1863. By January 1865, the addition of three new companies allowed the regiment to be created. George Tait was promoted to colonel and ordered to Asheville. Tait arrived on February 11. "Just at dark a munity broke out among the men," Tait wrote to Governor Vance, which resulted "in my being severely wounded and rendered insensible by a rock which struck me on the forehead. The insubordination exten[ded] to the whole command…and under no circumstance will I resume command of it. I cannot command a mob who would dare to strike you through me." Tait returned to Raleigh. Robert L. Coleman, then serving as commissary of subsistence for the District of Western North Carolina, was appointed colonel on March 2, 1865.[193]

Kirk's command was roaming all over the mountains. While the Confederate forces were out foraging, Kirk's men slunk into Mars Hill on March 8, burning the college buildings being used as a headquarters by Confederate forces. Even though the Third North Carolina Mounted Infantry (U.S.) was still not complete, Kirk was officially promoted to the rank of colonel on March 14, 1865. His men were spread out all over the mountain counties, recruiting, raiding and foraging for supplies. Robert W. Hubbard, who formerly had served in the First Ohio Heavy Artillery and was then serving as the first adjutant of the Third North Carolina, was promoted to lieutenant colonel. William W. Rollins, a South Carolina native, was appointed major of the regiment. Rollins previously served as a captain of the Twenty-Ninth North Carolina Troops. He deserted in August 1864, taking twenty men with him.[194]

Joseph G. Martin was assigned to command the Department of Western North Carolina. *North Carolina Museum of History.*

Confederate and Home Guard forces in Western North Carolina were falling apart. Brigadier General Joseph G. Martin, who had seen service in Eastern North Carolina and Virginia, was transferred to Western North Carolina in July 1864 and assumed command of the department. John B. Palmer took active command of the troops in the field. In March 1865, Martin split the district, as there was an ongoing feud between Thomas and Palmer. While Palmer was in command of troops in the field, Thomas refused to take orders from Palmer. Thomas was even arrested and sent to Richmond to answer the charges against him. Thomas's command encompassed the counties west of and including Haywood County, while Palmer commanded the counties east of Haywood. Major Stringfield wrote Colonel Thomas on February 21 about the condition of the Legion:

> *You will find Some day I fear*[,] *Col Thomas, a fearful and Shamful want of discipline on the part of a great many men & not a few officers of the Legion. This must be checked—destroyed—or our command is worthless when the hour of trial comes. In an election held in Cooper*[']*s Co*[.] *some time Since, a cowardly deserter by the name of Carver was elected Lieut. I now do most earnestly protest against this fellow retaining that place*[.] *I will not recognize him as an officer unless forced to do So, for I know from experience & observation that this fellow is bad at heart and cowardly by nature. I hope you will refuse to receive this fellow & order a new election*[;] *it will Save me the unpleasant duty of protesting before a higher tribunal.*
>
> *We already have Some men as officers who disgrace their uniform and I wish no more such. Col Love knows this man Carver & will coincide with me in protesting against his promotion. I do this all after mature reflection and with the Sincere desire to promote the good of the Service.*[195]

Things were little better with the Home Guard companies and battalions spread across the mountains. In the Banner Elk community of Watauga County, a man by the name of James Champion gathered about 25 members of the Thirteenth Tennessee Cavalry (U.S.), along with 50 other men, armed "with muskets, shotguns and hog rifles." Their objective was Camp Mast. They set out on the evening of February 4, proceeding to Valle Crucis, where they killed a cow and had supper. Champion told the men of his plans, advising that anyone "who expected to loot or rob or burn or destroy any property not strictly contraband, he must fall out." At that, 20 of the 123 men present slipped out into the darkness. Using James Isaacs as a guide, the band crossed Brushy Fork Creek at Vilas and arrived at the camp about dawn. The ground was frozen; they believed that "the clang of their horses' shoes had aroused every dog in Christendom, and just before reaching the camp a flock of sheep became frightened and fled helter-skelter down the ridge toward the camp." Yet the Home Guardsmen, possibly due to the weather, had failed to place a picket around their camp, an odd omission considering that the officer in charge had sent word to the other company in Boone that he expected an attack on the camp.

Champion divided his force into three sections. The men surrounded the camp, with every other man ordered to build a campfire. As the Home

Guard soldiers straggled from their cabins, they were greeted by the ring of fires in the early morning light. General H. Franklin, "a fine looking Yankee soldier", and a lieutenant in the Thirteenth Tennessee Cavalry (U.S.), stood on the hillside with a white flag. He headed into the camp, possibly escorted by Henry Lineback, also of the Thirteenth Cavalry, with a note for the commander, demanding the surrender of the camp. The Home Guardsmen had half an hour to decide, or Champion would attack. After polling the men, the camp's commander, Captain George McGuire, informed Champion that sixty men had voted to surrender, while eleven voted to stay and fight. The Home Guardsmen surrendered, and Champion ordered his men to burn the camp. Soon thereafter, Champion had his men and the prisoners back on the road, moving toward the Banner Elk settlement. It was recalled that the men "marched in pairs—two guards with guns, behind two prisoners, each with his blanket rolled and tied in a circle that passed over one shoulder and under one arm." When the other company arrived from Boone a little later, they discovered the men gone and the camp in smoking ruins. Many suspected that the company commander McGuire was complicit in the surrender, as he was seen riding away with the Federal officers. While that is possible, he simply could have been afforded the privilege of an honorable retreat because he was an officer.

The prisoners were split into two groups for the night, and local people prepared rations. Some of the prisoners, like brothers Silas and A.J. McBride, were able to steal away in the night. The remaining prisoners set out early the next morning, and upon reaching Shell Creek, just over the Tennessee line, those who had voted to surrender were paroled and released, allowed to return to their homes, while those who had voted to fight it out were escorted on to prison. Among those captured and sent to prison were local Confederate enrolling officer Lieutenant James H. Webb, Paul Farthing and his nephew Reuben Farthing, who were all sent to Camp Chase in Ohio. Webb was later paroled, but the Farthings both died of disease while incarcerated.[196]

Something larger than a raid on a single Home Guard camp was brewing. On the last day of January 1865, General Grant laid the groundwork for a much larger military operation. It was his suggestion that General George Stoneman take his cavalry and move toward Columbia, South Carolina, destroying the railroad and "military resources" that Sherman would not come close enough to destroy on his own march north. On Stoneman's return to East Tennessee, he might visit Salisbury, "releasing some of our prisoners of war in rebel hands." The purpose of Stoneman's raid was "to destroy and

Alvan C. Gillem's brigade contained several Tennessee regiments. *Library of Congress.*

not to fight battles." Stoneman, in turn, wrote to Gillem, informing him of his orders. These new directives, Stoneman believed, would allow Gillem's "fine body of Cossacks…to play a very important part." Gillem was ordered to start assembling his far-flung command.[197]

"Has Stoneman started on his raid?" an impatient Grant wrote on March 14. By the time Stoneman's troopers stepped off on March 21, the plans had changed. Sherman's Federal soldiers had already passed through South Carolina, entering the Tar Heel State east of Charlotte on March 3. Grant directed Stoneman to raid toward Lynchburg, Virginia, destroying the railroad, instead of moving into South Carolina. Rains delayed the arrival of Federal troops in Knoxville. It was Sherman's suggestion that Stoneman's directive again change: "Let Stoneman push toward Greensborough or Charlotte from Knoxville," he wrote to Grant. "Even a feint in that quarter will be more important. The railroad from Charlotte to Danville is all that is left to the enemy."[198]

A segment of the overall Federal cavalry force consisted of regiments made from local men, like the Eighth and Thirteenth Tennessee Cavalries and the Second and Third North Carolina Mounted Infantries. Other regiments came from Kentucky and Michigan. When the Federal cavalry reached Morristown, the troopers were greeted with a "cordial, hearty welcome from the loyal citizens....[P]eople came from all the surrounding country to see us and while perched on their rail fences greeted us with smiles." Hearing that there were Confederates in the vicinity of Jonesborough, Stoneman divided his forces. A portion moved toward Greeneville, while others continued toward Jonesborough. Along the route were minor skirmishes, but the Federals encountered little resistance. Confederate forces in the area concentrated between Bristol and Abington. East Tennessee was left in an "undefended vacuum," according to one historian. Parts of the Federal column were in Limestone on March 26, while the main body reached Elizabethton about the same time. The Federals stayed no place very long, but there were thousands of troopers filing past any given spot. The main column spent the evening near Butler, Tennessee, in Johnson County, establishing a signal post to relay messages back to other forces to the west.[199]

No farm was safe from Stoneman's men. Many years after the war, Finley Curtis Jr. told a story of when the Federals despoiled his family's Butler home. Curtis had sons in the Confederate army, including one who was lost at the Battle of Spotsylvania Court House in May 1864. The house was full of people, men, women and girls, and Curtis's father very ill. "Stoneman! Stoneman! was the dread name on every lip. Rumor said he was coming....Then suddenly, as if by some infernal prearrangement, the loud stamp of booted feet upon the front porch, deep guttural noises, violent knocks at the door." The family demanded to know what the troopers wanted. "Supper and—I, just anything," came the reply. The door was opened, and "two dozen or more" troopers filled the house. They swarmed over the rooms. At first, they attempted to enter the sick man's room. Tears from one of the daughters, explaining that he was very ill, kept the door closed for a while. Eventually, the Federal officer opened the door to the sick room, saw the mother asleep, the father in the bed and what appeared to be a doctor getting ready to administer medicine. The doctor was not a doctor but a Confederate soldier, home on furlough. The ruse worked, and the officer closed the door. Yet the others combed through the house. "If four people were ever ubiquitous, surely we were, my two sisters, myself, and young black Eliza—now in the kitchen…the parlor…the bedrooms…the halls and closets…upstairs…down[stairs], here and there, everywhere, begging to keep this and pleading to keep that, tearfully substituting, guarding, and secretly concealing every possible valuable." Their home had been robbed before, and they had devised places to conceal valuables, yet the family anxiously "watched these secret caches!" After taking what interested them from the house, the troopers headed for the barn, taking corn, wheat, rye and horses. "O how we hated…those Yankee vandals!" one of the sisters recalled as the family's horses were ridden down the muddy road into the darkness.[200]

People in the mountains had quickly grown adept at hiding valuables and foodstuffs. In the St. James community of Greene County, a woman, on seeing Rebel soldiers approaching her home, took to the bed. She told the raiders that she was sick. What she did not mention was that the family's last ham was in the bed with her. Matilda Jones, in Cocke County, recalled that her family hollowed out a log in their cabin, keeping most of the food within. Another Cocke County family, the Faubians, had part of the wall removed in an upstairs bedroom. This led to an empty space above the porch where valuables were hidden. The hole was recovered with boards, and a bed was moved up against the wall. In Yancey County, Jesse Bailey wrapped his pork in wax paper and took it to the woods to bury. As he was spreading dry leaves on the spot, a neighbor happened by. "Well, Uncle Jesse, I guess you are burying your meat," the neighbor commented. It was soon dug up and secreted in another location. On Indian Creek in Greasy Cove, Ann Tinker hid her husband's clothes and razor in a crevice between the chimney and the eaves of their cabin, while the foodstuff was buried. Philip Tinker was in the Confederate army, and when the raiders came, they stripped the house of its contents but did not get the hidden food or clothes. Sally Brown, of Watauga County, whose husband was in a prisoner-of-war camp in Maryland, started pulling the siding off her house and "crammed meat, grain, and dried food such as beans, dried fruits and vegetables between the walls, then nailed the boards back in place." Next, Brown put her good seed potatoes in the potato hole, covered them with straw and raked bad potatoes on top. When the Federals did arrive, they found no meat and only rotten potatoes. The David Greene family on Stony Fork Creek in eastern Watauga County had a trapdoor in one room that led to a hidden cellar. The family kept their food in the cellar during the war. In Jonesborough, a pair of families who shared differing political beliefs worked out an ingenious solution. When Union soldiers were in town, the Southern family passed their prized possessions to the Unionist family through the attic. The objects were returned once the danger had passed. Likewise, the Unionist family passed the objects through the attic and down to the other family when Confederate soldiers were in town.[201]

Livestock was always highly sought by regular soldiers and opportunistic raiders. In Greene County, the Russell women hid their livestock in a nearby sinkhole. A Cocke County family dug a cellar under their home to hide their livestock, while another family hid their horses in the basement of Beechwood Hall. Watauga County's Alfred Adams recalled hiding a yoke of oxen in a hollow near his family home.[202]

Sometimes, raiders or soldiers appeared with little notice. In Cocke County, raiders appeared at the farm of Dorcas Smith, whose husband was away serving in the Union army. The cabin was stripped of food, which was piled up in the yard. When the thieves went to catch the chickens, she quickly climbed on top of the pile and urinated on the food. The raiders reportedly left in disgust, and Dorcas cleaned the food and stored it away. A neighbor was cleaning a chicken when soldiers suddenly appeared. The lady quickly dunked the fowl in a slop bucket. When the frustrated soldiers rode on, she fished the bird out, cleaned it and cooked it. In Watauga County, Joe Mast was working at his gristmill on Cove Creek. When word came that Stoneman's men were approaching, Mast's daughters took his horses into the woods and hid until the threat had passed. Mast himself slipped away, and the Federals took everything at the mill except one bag of ground meal that Mast's daughter Fronia hid by sitting on it and covering it with her skirt.[203]

Early on the morning of March 28, Stoneman's lead elements crossed over the Iron Mountains and into Watauga County. A detachment of the Twelfth Kentucky Cavalry, under Major Myles Keogh, moved toward Boone. It is possible that the first person with whom they came into contact was Jacob Councill. According to an account written not too many years after the war, Councill "was plowing with a negro. He was…a prudent,

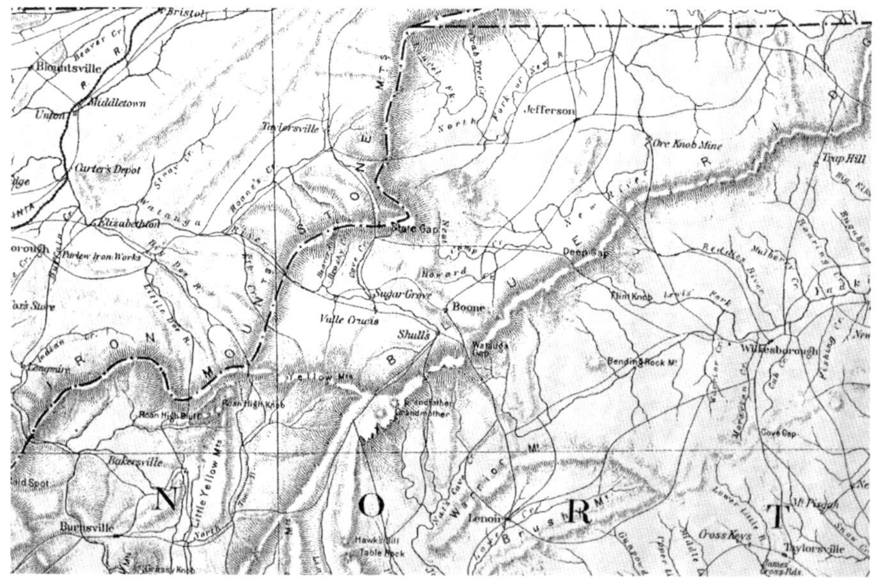

The hard hand of war visited Watauga County and the surrounding area when Kirk's regiments arrived in April 1865. *Author's collection.*

quiet man….He was shot down in cold blood, notwithstanding his piteous cries for mercy, because, upon the negro's statement, he was 'an infernal rebel.'" Another account states that Councill was in the act of putting away his harness when he came to the door and was shot and killed. While there is nothing to confirm Councill's being an "infernal rebel," he was a thirty-five-year-old father of at least three children, not a slave owner, but was a member of the Home Guard.[204]

That Tuesday morning, the Home Guard was assembled in Boone. It had been more than a month since Camp Mast had been captured. Seeing the blue-coated cavalrymen ride into Boone from the west, some Home Guardsmen fled, while others went into the house of James W. Councill, where they opened fire on the Kentucky soldiers. A few later wrote that they thought it was James Hartley's gang, and they were not going to be duped like they had been at the surrender of Camp Mast. The Federal cavalry opened fire and charged into the town. Hearing the commotion, Mary Councill, holding one of her children, stepped out on the front porch of her home. She was greeted by "a volley of balls[that] splintered the wood-work all around her" but escaped back inside unhurt. The rest of the Home Guard scattered, with the Federal cavalry in hot pursuit. John Bryan was "struck by a soldier…with

George Stoneman was ordered by General Grant to raid through North Carolina in 1865. *Library of Congress.*

a gun." John Brown's ankle was broken, while Thomas Holder was wounded in the hip and groin. Andrew J. McBride, who had escaped after being captured at Camp Mast, was shot in the breast, "the ball followed a rib and lodged near his spine." Calvin Greene had attempted to surrender but was fired upon. So he retrieved his rifle "and fought, loading and firing till he was shot down and left for dead…[shattering] the arm of one of the Federal soldiers." Warren Greene "was killed while holding up his hands in token of surrender." Also killed was Ephraim Norris, who was just shy of his forty-sixth birthday. Others, like fifteen-year-old Steel Frazier, continued to fight on, although the account of his killing at least one of his pursuers is possibly exaggerated. The "Battle of Boone" was actually just a mere skirmish, lasting but a few moments. Federals swarmed the town, and Stoneman's men arrested just about every male in the vicinity. The number of captured was reported as sixty-eight. The local jail, along with a majority of the court records, was burned.[205]

Stoneman split his command. A portion traveled through Deep Gap and into Wilkes County, while another brigade moved through Blowing Rock and into Caldwell County. In the Patterson community of Caldwell County, the local mill that made blankets was burned. The troopers then turned toward Wilkes County, moving along the Yadkin River. Stoneman eventually made his way back into Virginia. His troopers returned to North Carolina on April 9, capturing Winston and Salem and skirmishing with Confederates at Shallow Ford and Mocksville. On April 12, Stoneman's troopers soundly defeated Confederates in a battle at Salisbury, but at Fort York, an entrenchment protecting the railroad bridge over the Yadkin River on the Davidson and Rowan County lines, Stoneman met stiff resistance. After failing to destroy the bridge, Federal troops turned back west, destroying supply depots in Salisbury and Statesville, before moving toward Lenoir.

Sometime around March 29 or 30, Daniel Ellis, now commanding a company in the Thirteenth Tennessee Cavalry (U.S.), learned of a

Confederate force in Elizabethton. The Thirteenth Tennessee Cavalry was a part of Stoneman's command moving east, but Ellis and a portion of his company were evidently left to protect Union people in the area. The Confederates, mostly members of Company C, Fifty-Ninth Tennessee, were apparently in Elizabethton, looking for Ellis's band. Ellis wrote that he had his men up early, dividing them into three squads. As they entered the town, a local citizen bellowed, "The Yankees are coming," alerting the Confederates. Some of the Confederates made for the courthouse, while others mounted and headed for the river. Ellis and a few others gave chase, crossing the river. Since his horse was faster than the others, Ellis outpaced his comrades and found himself face-to-face with a couple of enemy soldiers. "[O]ne of them presented his gun and burst a cap at me, saying 'I will kill you, you damned scoundrel!' I thought I could see half way down the barrel of his gun, for we were not more than five steps apart," Ellis later claimed. Ellis leapt from his horse and struck the man in the head with his pistol. He caught another, and a third escaped. The man Ellis struck was attempting to recap his pistol. "I immediately let the one go that I was holding and knocked him down again, and then grasped hold of the other man a second time." More of Ellis's men begin to arrive, and the soldier attempting to shoot Ellis was killed. The group took their prisoners to an old house up in the mountains for a few days before sending them on to Knoxville. Ellis claimed they killed three Confederates and captured eleven during the Battle of Elizabethton. Edward Guerrant, a Confederate staff officer serving in the area, wrote that the skirmish took place on March 28, 1865, and that thirty men were captured. The compiled service records of several men captured are not as clear. Isaac Bowers, a member of the Fifty-Ninth Tennessee, was reported captured in Boone on March 28, in Carter County on March 30 and in Carter County again on March 31. By April 30, Bowers was at Camp Chase in Ohio. He was not released until June 10, 1865, after he took the Oath of Allegiance.[206]

To protect his line of retreat, Stoneman ordered the Second and Third North Carolina Mounted Infantry (U.S.), both under the command of Colonel Kirk, into Watauga County. Kirk set out on April 5, possibly from Limestone Cove, moving through Crab Orchard and Banner Elk. The two regiments arrived in Boone on April 6. Kirk established his headquarters in Boone at the Councill home, keeping just over four hundred men with him. On April 7, Major Andrew Bahney was ordered to take portions of the Second North Carolina Mounted Infantry to Deep Gap, while Major William Rollins took a portion of the Third North Carolina Mounted Infantry to

This conceptual illustration shows Ellis battling with Confederate soldiers south of Elizabethton. *From* The Thrilling Adventures of Daniel Ellis.

Blowing Rock. Furthermore, Kirk was ordered to blockade both Sampson Gap and the Meat Camp Road. Boone, Deep Gap and Watauga Gap near Blowing Rock were all fortified. In Boone, Kirk ordered holes cut into the walls of the courthouse to provide firing ports, while three frame dwelling houses and a log smokehouse owned by John "Jack" Horton were dismantled and used to build a barricade around the courthouse. Ironically, Horton was a Unionist, but like his more Confederate sympathizing neighbors, he was indiscriminately preyed upon by the invaders. The stronghold in Deep Gap was "a palisade fort enclosing about an acre and ditched around." At Watauga Gap, the Federals also built works, possibly dismantling the summer home of Caldwell County resident James Harper, while at the same time cutting down trees to provide better observation points. The Federal soldiers named this work Fort Rollins, in honor of their major. These works were all constructed both to help protect Stoneman's rear and to keep open a line of retreat if it were needed.[207]

Since the majority of Kirk's men were from the area, and because many had been hunted heavily by the Home Guard, their retribution on the citizenry was vicious. They moved out in small bands to steal and requisition from the local population. "They came to our home every day to commandeer what they could find," recalled Alfred Adams. The home of Jonathan and Malinda Horton was robbed eighteen times in fourteen days. Sarah Johnson was out plowing "with an old scrawny horse" when the Federals arrived. The soldiers demanded that Mrs. Johnson unhitch the horse. She replied to their commander that "if he touched the horse she'd beat his brains out" with a hoe she was holding. After sizing up the situation, the Federal commander was rumored to have told his men to leave the horse, "because I'd have to kill the old fool and the horse ain't worth it." Even those who professed to be Union men were not immune to the ravages of Kirk's men. Rittenhouse Baird was out plowing when five Federal soldiers came and relieved him of his horse, saddle and bridle. Joshua Horton stated that he lost seven hundred pounds of bacon, fifty bushels of corn, twenty-five bushels of potatoes and thirty chickens, along with four thousand fence rails. William Vandyke lost one horse. John "Jack" Horton claimed not only losing the three houses and the smokehouse that were used to fortify the courthouse in Boone but also a wagon jack and harness, a mule, four saddles, seven stacks of hay, two wagons, twenty bushels of corn, three hundred pounds of bacon and a great deal of leather, not to mention fence rails taken and burned for the campfires of soldiers. Horton applied to the Federal government for reimbursement after the war, claiming $1,553.20 in damages, but he was only awarded $512.00.

Albert Wilson was at home when the raiders came through and recalled later that he "saw the houses of his neighbors burned and sacked."[208]

Watauga County was not the only objective of Kirk's plans. A band of raiders, most from Kirk's command, roamed through Yancey County as well. They stopped at the residence of Sam Byrd Sr. His son was commander of the Home Guard battalion. A few weeks earlier, the Home Guard had caught and killed Mack McCurry while he was attempting to cross the mountains and join the Union army. The raiders were looking for the younger Byrd or the weapons that were rumored to have been kept at the home. A slave saw the raiders coming and gave warning. The senior Byrd climbed into the loft, removed a notch in the logs and warned the group not to pass beyond the gate. Words passed between Byrd and the raiders, and one of them attempted to walk through the gate. John Bennett was shot in the side when Byrd made good on his threat, and he died on April 20. The raiders then set fire to the back side of the cabin, telling Byrd that if he came out, the fire would be extinguished. Byrd came out and was shot over twenty times. The fire was quenched and the home robbed. At some point, Kirk's raiders ventured on to Burnsville, setting fire to the old academy building. They also robbed the home of local Unionist Samuel Honeycutt, taking his horse. More than just raiding was taking place, as theft devolved rapidly into violence and wanton destruction.[209]

General Stoneman was back in Watauga County on April 17 with a large number of Confederate prisoners. One prisoner estimated the total number at over one thousand. Those prisoners were quartered in Blowing Rock for a night. At some point, several of them attempted to escape into a mountain laurel thicket alongside the road. The guards fired on the band; a Captain Price of Virginia was badly wounded, and he was left behind. Lieutenant John T. Shotwell also ran, and as he was attempting to surrender, Colonel Kirk was heard to say, "D--n him, shoot him!" This order was carried out. "[T]his gallant young man was murdered right before our eyes and left lying as he had fallen," recalled a fellow prisoner. "A friend of his begged to be allowed to go to him and when permission was given, he went and straightened his body and took fifty dollars in gold, intending to send it to young Shotwell's father, but was soon relieved of it by an officer." The prisoners continued to Boone and were possibly quartered in the stockade built around the courthouse. One prisoner recalled that "Kirk rode into our midst, called us 'cowards, cut-throats, damned rebels,' and every vile thing he could think of, and threatened the most horrible vengeance if we attempted to escape." Stoneman spent the night with the Councill family once again. Whereas Stoneman had been kind

Federal forces under Kirk entrenched several places in Watauga County, including Deep Gap. *Author's collection.*

to Mrs. Councill, in deference to the fact that she had often fed Federal prisoners at the jail in Boone, Kirk had kept the family locked in their rooms. Stoneman, "standing in the piazza and taking survey of what had once been a happy and beautiful home," now found "the fencing all gone, the gardens, shrubbery, and yard trampled bare, covered with raw hides of cattle and sheep, decaying carcasses, and all manner of filth." Stoneman left the following day, heading back west into Tennessee. His thousand prisoners moved to the west as well, camping the next night at the head of Cove Creek and the following night at Dugger's Forge in Carter County, Tennessee. Rations were not issued to the prisoners until they reached Greeneville, where they were finally given hardtack and bacon.[210]

Stoneman did not return, but his command continued to move west. His men pushed through Lenoir. The Federals skirmished successfully with local troops at Rocky Ford on the Catawba River, and soon Morganton was in Federal hands. After pillaging the town, the Federals continued toward Asheville. On April 20, they found Swannanoa Gap obstructed and set about flanking the position, moving through Rutherfordton on April 21. Confederate forces blockading Swannanoa Gap were ordered to Howard's Gap, eight miles north. Many, however, refused to comply, hearing rumors that surrender negotiations were in progress.[211]

Federal soldiers had already attempted to capture Asheville. On April 3, several Ohio regiments, recently transferred from Virginia to East Tennessee, set out on a "scout in the direction of Asheville." A member of the regiment wrote after the war that the "depredations of guerrillas, bushwhackers and similar assassins had become so serious that it was decided to send a force into northwestern North Carolina, to intimidate, and...punish them." The Ohioans crossed the Nolichucky Creek and picked up the road to North Carolina ten miles below Greeneville. At Paint Rock, on the North Carolina–Tennessee border, twenty-five men were left to hold the pass. The brigade, numbering about nine hundred men, camped in Warm Springs that evening. Their route had been a rough one. As they moved down the French Broad, their path was obstructed by felled trees, with "stumps and logs and rocks that had been rolled down from the hill-sides." Asheville was prepared. As early as February 1864, breastworks had been dug, with emplacements for cannons. However, Asheville had few troops to man those works. Palmer's brigade, composed of the remnants of the Sixty-Second and Sixty-Fourth North Carolina Troops, with a battery from South Carolina, along with a few Home Guard members, were all the soldiers to be had.[212]

Continuing their advance on the morning of April 6, Colonel Isaac Kirby, commanding the expedition, complained that guerrillas were "firing… from trees, stumps, rocks, etc." Kirby sent his artillery and supply wagons back to Warm Springs. As they neared the town, a Federal staff officer with a few mounted men dashed into the edge of Asheville, capturing five Confederates and a wagon with its team. "The enemy could be seen forming a line of battle in the far part of the town," a staff officer wrote a few days later. "One bright day, while we were at dinner, the beating of the long roll commenced and soon every man was in line," Beverly Morris, a member of the Sixty-Fourth, wrote many years later. "Colonel Palmer was commanding and formed a line of battle on the top of a ridge between our camp and the River road." Kirby had no idea how many men he faced. His advance was already engaged with the Confederates when he reached the field. He deployed the rest of his brigade and pushed forward his skirmishers, driving back the Confederate skirmishers. At this point, he discovered Confederates working their way around his rear, trying to cut off his line of retreat. "I was compelled to change position and examine more closely the position of the enemy," Kirby wrote. "I found him occupying two very high hills, which were very difficult of approach with my small force."[213]

Morris reported that the Federals actually threw up defensive works themselves and opened fire, the "Yankee balls passing over our men and rattling on our shanties." Midafternoon, Morris's regiment was moved forward and then engaged in a "game of bluff." One company was passed through a gap several times, in sight of the Federals. Prisoners who had fallen into Kirby's command reported a Confederate force of at least one thousand men, with six cannons and "400 or 500 more men from the south side of the river" who could reinforce his band. The Federals held their position until that evening, when Morris used the cover of darkness and a rainstorm to mask his withdrawal. A local citizen recalled years later that the route of the retreat was littered with "abandoned guns, bayonets, canteens,

This small plaque marks one of the breastworks dug to protect Asheville during the war. *Author's collection.*

pocket knives, and other articles of army equipment whose loss indicated a hasty departure by their recent owners." One Ohio veteran recalled that the march from Alexander's Bridge began at two o'clock in the morning, reaching Marshall at nine. "From this point," the veteran wrote, "our march was deliberate." Kirby had his brigade back in Greeneville by April 10. He reported no killed and only two seriously wounded. Confederate losses were about the same.[214]

Stoneman's troopers continued to work their way west toward Asheville. The two forces skirmished at Howard's Gap on April 21. On April 23, the Federal and Confederate commanders met near Asheville. Brigadier General James Martin rode out to meet Gillem on April 24, just south of Asheville. They agreed to honor the truce worked out between Joseph E. Johnston and William T. Sherman near Durham a few days earlier. Gillem was planning to move his command into South Carolina and asked Martin for rations and forage. Martin agreed to give the Federals nine thousand rations but had no forage to spare. Local citizens thought Martin's request for rations "almost impossible" but managed to fill the order. Gillem had told Martin that the rations would prevent "the necessity of stripping the citizens of their scant supplies."

Some of Gillem's forces moved toward South Carolina, and the others were returning to Tennessee.[215]

Federal cavalry rode through the streets of Asheville on April 25. Earlier in the war, Andrew Johnson had considered Asheville a "damned secession hole in the mountains." The town was the largest in the western part of the state. Numerous companies for Confederate service had come from the area, along with Governor Vance. For part of the war, there had been an armory in Asheville, manufacturing rifles. The town also had a hospital, prison and training camps. Many of the dissidents captured in Yancey, Madison and farther west spent time in the prison in Asheville. "A large force of Yankee cavalry passed through as quietly as if they were not on hostile soil," one resident noted. However, a member of the Thirteenth Tennessee Cavalry (U.S.) noted that the Confederate soldiers, after stacking their arms, had lined the sides of the streets, and the two forces were "guying each other."[216]

About ten miles north of Asheville, Federal cavalrymen went into camp. The next day, they reached Marshall. Gillem was delayed, due to the road along the French Broad being blocked. As the troopers looked for an alternative, word reached them that the armistice between Johnston and Sherman had fallen apart and Lincoln had been assassinated. Gillem was ordered to destroy the railroad bridges over the Catawba River and to establish his headquarters in Asheville. Gillem placed the column under the command of William J. Palmer and then rode for Greeneville. Reaching Asheville on the evening of April 26, the Federals promptly surrounded the town and demanded its surrender. Martin tried to hold his position but was simply overwhelmed. There was some skirmishing in the streets, but Asheville quickly fell. "We were surprised and almost panic stricken by their return as a devastating mob, to capture and sack our unprotected homes," one of Martin's staff officers later chronicled. "I have heard of no worse plundering any where than was permitted in & near Asheville," Martin wrote. Martin was arrested and then released an hour later. As he neared his residence, "I found Mrs Martin & my daughter going into the house with a squad of Federal soldiers holding candles…for them to examine all the trunks &c for such things as they fancied & to such things they helped themselves." Martin's escort ordered the soldiers to leave, and the Federal officer remained himself to ensure the house was secure. There were several hundred men captured. They were confined in two local warehouses before being sent back toward Tennessee. One resident noted that the Federal troopers "threatened to burn the whole town." The Stars and Stripes floated over the street.[217]

Stoneman's command soon moved south, ordered to pursue Jefferson Davis and the remnants of the Confederate government heading from Charlotte and into South Carolina. On April 23, Kirk was ordered to leave his base in Watauga County and move toward Warm Springs. For the residents of Watauga County, it was none too soon. From Lenoir, Robert Beall wrote that "Kirk's men seemed to have a special spite of Boone and the citizens of Watauga County." Kirk left no official report, so the movements of his regiments are vague. They are believed to have moved through Lenoir and into Morganton, where they raided the town. Miller's brigade of Stoneman's command was ordered to remain behind in Asheville, while Kirk's men swept the area between Asheville and the Tennessee line. Martin, and what Confederate troops he could muster, left Asheville on April 29, the day before Miller's brigade arrived. Martin placed two hundred men under Colonel Love at Balsam Gap and about two hundred more men under Thomas at Soco Gap. Martin ordered Lieutenant Robert Conley to take a company and reinforce Love's men at Balsam Gap. On May 6, near White Sulphur Springs, Conley ran into a portion of the Second North Carolina Mounted Infantry (U.S.). The skirmish was quick, and a man named Arrowood was reportedly killed, although this later proved untrue. The Federal troopers quickly retreated, and the skirmish is frequently referred to as the last battle east of the Mississippi River.[218]

News of the skirmish reached Martin, who was in Webster. He was determined to capture the Federals who had retreated to Waynesville. Thomas employed his men in building numerous fires on the surrounding hillsides and throughout the night had them beat drums while "making…hideous…ear splitting war whoops." The Federal commander, Lieutenant Colonel William Bartlett, sent a flag of truce out the next morning, and he met with Martin, Thomas and Love. According to one story, Thomas brought twenty of his Cherokee warriors with him, "stripped to the waist and *painted and feathered in good old style.*" Thomas threatened the Federal soldiers with scalping if they did not surrender. Martin soon intervened and agreed to surrender all the troops in Western North Carolina under his command. In return, Bartlett would convey a message to Kirk: his forces would cease robbing people, return stolen property and leave the area. With the terms agreed upon, troops in Waynesville surrendered. Confederate soldiers present, save Thomas's personal bodyguard, signed parole papers and went home.[219]

Kirk was ordered to block the passes between Rabun Gap and Swannanoa Gap, watching for bushwhackers and closing the area to

The monument commemorating the "Last Shot of the Civil War" was erected near Waynesville in 1923. *North Carolina Division of Archives and History.*

Jefferson Davis's party as the Confederate leadership attempted to avoid capture in the waning days of the war. William Palmer recommended that his men be sent back to East Tennessee, "to prevent his men from pillaging and committing excesses." Kirk was still in Macon County on May 12, where a portion of Thomas's Legion surrendered at Franklin. This was regarded by some as the last surrender of Confederate troops east of the Mississippi River. Kirk's Third North Carolina Mounted Infantry arrived in Asheville on May 17. They continued to do garrison duty and rounded up deserters for the next few weeks. Daniel Ellis was likewise ordered to sweep through East Tennessee, arresting deserters from whatever Federal regiments he could find. He returned with "a motley assemblage" of 125 men and forty horses, including Federal deserters, Confederate deserters and members of the "hated home guards," hoping to avoid whatever awaited their comrades back at home in the mountains. In July, Kirk applied for leave to attend to personal matters in Charlotte. On August 8, 1865, Kirk and the remaining members of the Third North Carolina Mounted Infantry (U.S.) were mustered out of the U.S. Army.[220]

In the mountain region, the war had truly been one in which brother fought against brother. Harvey Bingham, commanding the Home Guard battalion in Watauga County, had lost one brother in a skirmish in 1864. Another brother, Thomas, had crossed the mountains and joined the Third Tennessee Mounted Infantry (U.S.) in September 1864. They both survived the war. The Crow brothers from neighboring Carter County also demonstrate the struggle between family and military loyalty. Christopher Crow was a private in the Forty-Third Tennessee Infantry. After the Battle of Blountville, his body was discovered by the Federals. Word was passed along to his brother John Crow, a private in the Thirteenth Tennessee Cavalry (U.S.), who was at the time driving an ambulance. After spending a few moments with his brother's body, John hired someone to bury Christopher and moved on with the rest of the army. Many never knew what became of their loved ones. Leander Pyatte lived near the Linville River. Pyatte had slipped home to repair the shoes of his children one night in December 1863 when he was captured by the Home Guard. By January 10, 1864, Pyatte was dead in a hospital in Atlanta. His descendants did not learn the details of his demise until the early 2000s.[221]

6

Postwar

"Take Your Damn Family...and Never Come Back Here Again"

It is easy to say that the Civil War ended with the surrenders of Lee's army at Appomattox and of Johnston's army at the Bennett Place, both in April 1865. Yet the war in the mountains continued to rage. Thousands of people were displaced by the war. Some were driven out by one of the armies. Others chose to abandon the area of their own accord. Hundreds more had their homes and farms destroyed. Adeline Deaderick recalled that "no distinction was made, as to Union, or Southern family." Her family's farm was visited numerous times during the war. The Deaderick family was eventually forced to leave their home and find refuge in Jonesborough. They found a neighbor who still had horses, loaded their wagon and rode off. "[L]ook for the last time on your home," Adeline's husband said, "for we will never come back to it….[I]t is associated in my mind with everything that is horrible…Murder, thefts, and midnight marauders." Even as the end came for the larger war, there was no peace in the mountains. A year after the surrender, the Deadericks received a note stating that they had to leave Jonesborough within ten days, "or death would be the 'penalty.'" A few days later, their house was surrounded and seven armed men entered, one of whom held a pistol to James Deaderick's head. When he asked his assailants why he should leave, their response was that he had helped Confederate authorities conscript local men for the army. Deaderick himself was a Union man, although he had sons in the Confederate army. He eventually agreed to depart. He had no wish to "stay with men, that did not want him." "[T]ake your damn family…and never come back here again," was the reply.

The family was soon gone. In 1870, James Deaderick became a justice on the Tennessee Supreme Court.[222]

Landon Carter Haynes, a Washington County lawyer and state representative, also left the region. Haynes was appointed one of the two Confederate senators from Tennessee, and when he was not in Richmond, he made his home in Knoxville. When Knoxville fell, he moved his family to Wytheville, Virginia. Once Richmond succumbed to Federal forces, he made his way to Statesville, North Carolina. The Haynes family lost their farm in Washington County and eventually settled in Memphis. Harvey Bingham, the Home Guard commander in Watauga County, also had to leave at the end of the war. He had done his job of collecting deserters and conscription evaders so well that he earned the enmity of his neighbors. Bingham moved to Statesville, where he practiced law and ran a law school until his death.[223]

Military actions also continued to erupt. A group of Federal deserters, largely from the Tenth Michigan Cavalry, took up residence at Fort Hamby, a home in western Wilkes County. From there, they continued to rob and plunder in nearby counties. Several attempts were made by locals to rout the men from their stronghold. Finally, a group of former Confederate soldiers, possibly numbering "several hundred men," attacked the fort, eventually setting fire to the log structure. Several of the renegades were caught and executed on the spot. In Cocke County, Unionists told Robert Roadman to leave or he would be killed. The Roadman home had been used to administer Confederate loyalty oaths to Unionists during the war. Roadman hated to give up his farm and tannery but chose to relocate. William Stringfield recalled meeting with Parson Brownlow not long after the war was over. When Stringfield confessed that he was going to leave East Tennessee because of the whippings of former Confederates by mobs, Brownlow advised him to stay but also to carry two pistols with him at all times. "[U]se them if necessary," Brownlow counseled Stringfield. In Washington County, a group of Union veterans attempted to kill a man suspected of abusing other Unionists during the war. Likewise, local secessionists claimed that two pro-Confederate men had been killed and two women raped.[224]

Some soldiers came heartbreakingly close to making it home. Haywood County's Allen Nolan served in both the Sixteenth North Carolina Troops and Thomas's Legion. He was discharged in Knoxville and was told to go home via Warm Springs and Asheville, as the Smokies were full of deserter gangs. Nolan was last seen alive on the top of Mount Sterling. His widow moved with their children into her parents' home.[225]

In 1889, Robert Farthing, speaking to Confederate veterans in Watauga County, stated that he believed that "the days of reconstruction" were "worse than the war if possible." For the next four or five years, there were clashes between the differing sides. In late 1865, Yancey County's James Sheenan was ordered to the Rowan County jail for ten days. His offense? Disrespecting an officer of the United States in the discharge of his duty. Six months later, it was reported that there were indictments issued against former Union soldiers and citizens in Yancey County. Matters were so heated that the judge had to call out the militia to preserve order. In East Tennessee, local Unionists were the ones indicting Confederates. William Stringfield was charged with burning a field in Carter County in 1862, while serving as provost marshal. One Cocke County man filed suit against a former Confederate for trespassing. The defendant had seized a gun under an act passed by the state legislature in November 1861. The state supreme court affirmed the lower court's decision: all ordinances passed after May 6, 1861, by the legislature were declared null and void. Besides civil litigation, there were also attempts to bring criminal cases against many former Confederates. Colonel George N. Folk, commanding a small number of troops in the raid at Fish Springs, was indicted for murder after the war. Folk, a respected Caldwell County lawyer who represented William Blalock in a postwar murder case, apparently never stood trial. There were 2,014 indictments for treason in Tennessee in 1865. "These men deserve to be punished, and even disfranchised, for they are guilty of treason to the State, the United States, and of perjury," Parson Brownlow wrote. Cocke County's John Wood was one of those. Wood was charged with supplying the Confederates, providing "100 horse, 1,000 pds of bacon, 1,000 bushels of corn, 100 hogs, 100 head cattle" to "false traitors." The indictment went as far as to accuse him of "being moved and seduced by the instigation of the devil." When it was proven that these indicted men had taken the Amnesty Oath, the charges were dropped.[226]

The lives of some of the principal participants best illustrate the lives of people after the war.

Robert B. Vance was captured on January 14, 1864, in Cocke County, Tennessee. He was incarcerated for a while at Fort Delaware and was eventually released on March 10, 1864. After returning to North Carolina, he served in the General Assembly, and then the U.S. House of Representatives from 1872 through 1884. For the next four years, Vance was an assistant commissioner of patents in Washington, D.C., and then again served in the North Carolina General Assembly. Vance was a member of the Methodist

Church and the Free Masons, founded a national temperance organization and was a noted lecturer and author. On November 28, 1899, Vance died in Buncombe County, and he is buried in Riverside Cemetery, Asheville.[227]

Zebulon Baird Vance, Robert's younger brother, was arrested by Union soldiers in Statesville on May 13, 1865. It was his thirty-fifth birthday. After his release, Vance practiced law in Charlotte. He was elected to the U.S. Senate in 1870, but due to restrictions placed on former Confederates by the Fourteenth Amendment of the Constitution, Vance was not allowed to serve. Vance was elected governor of North Carolina in 1876 and then became a U.S. senator in 1879. He continued to serve until his death in Washington, D.C., in 1894. Vance is interred in Riverside Cemetery in Asheville.[228]

John B. Palmer, colonel of the Fifty-Eighth North Carolina Troops, was sent to replace Robert B. Vance. He spent the rest of the war in Western North Carolina and East Tennessee. His Compiled Service Records state he was captured in Athens, Georgia, on May 8, 1865. After his release, Palmer first went to Rutherfordton, then on to Columbia, South Carolina. Palmer became vice president of two different banks and then president of two different railroads: the Charlotte, Columbia and Augusta Railroad and then the Atlantic Coast Line. Palmer sold his property along the Linville River

Governor Zebulon B. Vance lies interred just behind his brother, Brigadier General Robert Vance, in Riverside Cemetery. *Author's collection.*

and spent his time in Richmond, Virginia, central Florida and Europe. He died on December 10, 1893, and is buried in Elmwood Cemetery in Columbia, South Carolina.

James Green Martin replaced Palmer as commander of the Department of Western North Carolina, while Palmer assumed command in the field. Martin hailed from Eastern North Carolina and, in 1840, graduated from West Point. After fighting in Mexico, Martin was stationed mostly out west. At first, Martin commanded North Carolina State Troops. In 1862, he was appointed a brigadier general in the Provisional Confederate Army. His brigade served in Eastern North Carolina and Virginia. Poor health forced him from brigade command, and he was assigned to Western North Carolina. Martin was paroled at Waynesboro on May 10. After the war, he became a successful lawyer and active layman in the Episcopal Church. General Martin died on October 4, 1878, and is interred in Riverside Cemetery, Asheville.[229]

George Stoneman's connection with the Western North Carolina–Tennessee border area was confined to the last year of the war. Amazingly enough, he was a classmate of James Green Martin. After the war, Stoneman served as military commander of Virginia and then in Tennessee. He was known for his moderate policies and even joined the Democratic Party. Stoneman was assigned command of the Department of Arizona and, in May 1871, was relieved of command. Settling in California, he served as governor from 1882 to 1886. Stoneman returned to New York for medical treatment and died of a stroke in Buffalo on September 5, 1894. He is buried in the Bentley Cemetery, Lakewood, New York.[230]

Daniel Ellis, also known as the "Old Red Fox," was born in Carter County, Tennessee, in December 1827. Ellis served as a guide for most of the war, finally joining the Thirteenth Tennessee Cavalry on January 13, 1865. He was mustered in as captain of Company A and mustered out with the regiment in September 1865. Ellis is best known for his 1867 book, *The Thrilling Adventures of Daniel Ellis, the Great Union Guide of East Tennessee for a Period of Nearly Four Years During the Great Southern Rebellion*. However, many of the "Thrilling Adventures" that Ellis describes cannot be substantiated. He was also extremely partisan. His neighbors were "infernal rebels," "inhuman devils," "merciless rebels," "black-hearted scoundrels," "blood-thirsty lions" and "blood-thirsty minions of Jeff. Davis and his compeers in wickedness." A wagon maker prior to the war, Ellis struggled after the end. He was awarded back pay for two years, but when he tried to file a claim to be compensated for horses lost during the war, he was turned down. The horses were not actually his but either ones he had taken from his Confederate-sympathizing neighbors or some of Morgan's men's mounts that he claimed to have captured. Ellis died on January 6, 1908, and is buried near Elizabethton, Tennessee.[231]

Daniel Ellis has a Tennessee Historical Marker at Valley Forge in Carter County. *Author's collection.*

William and Malinda Blalock both survived the war, but the conflict was not over for them. On his discharge, Blalock purchased a rifle and, in February 1866, shot and killed John Boyd in Caldwell County. Blalock turned himself in but was later pardoned by Republican governor William Holden. The Blalocks went to Texas, and possibly Oregon, before returning to Bakersville in Mitchell County. They eventually settled in the Montezuma community of present-day Avery County. Malinda died in 1903, and William died in 1913. Both are buried in the Montezuma Community Cemetery.

Andrew Johnson was Lincoln's running mate in 1864 and became vice president of the United States. Upon Lincoln's death, he ascended to the presidency. He took it upon himself to pardon all who would take an oath of allegiance, except leaders and men of wealth; they had to obtain a special presidential pardon. When prewar Southern leaders began to resume their offices, the Radical Republican Congress stepped in, passing various acts that Johnson vetoed. Those vetoes were overturned. Johnson believed that there was no need for Reconstruction: Southern states could not truly depart from the Union in the first place. With his clashes between the Radicals and lacking the backing of the Democrats, Johnson's time as president was fraught with political perils. He was not nominated for a second term and returned home to Greeneville in 1869. Johnson was elected to another term in the U.S. Senate in 1875 but died at the home of his daughter in Carter County on July 31, 1875. He is interred in Greeneville, Tennessee.

George W. Kirk, after his discharge from the army, presumably went back home to Greene County and resumed his prewar occupations of farming and carpentry. From time to time, Kirk popped up in local newspapers.

In March 1867, he was recommended to command a company to go into McMinn County to put down "rebels and copperheads." In May 1867, he was in Jonesborough, attending a "Grand Rally of Radical Unionists." Kirk may have led a company of state guards during some of the early conflicts with the Ku Klux Klan. Back in North Carolina, Governor William W. Holden was having his own problems with violence. He also chose to raise a state militia to go into several counties and crush the dissidents. At first, he offered command of one of the two regiments he raised to William Rollins, former major of the Third North Carolina Mounted Infantry. Rollins, however, then practicing law in Madison County, declined and recommended Kirk for the job. Kirk raised a regiment made up of East Tennessee and Western North Carolina men and marched into the Tar Heel State. In Caswell County, Kirk arrested a number of local men and detained them at his camp. When North Carolina chief justice Richmond Pearson directed writs of habeas corpus be issued, Holden countered the order. Finally, a federal judge in Salisbury ordered most of the prisoners released. In September 1870, Holden declared the insurrection over, and the militia was disbanded. Holden was then impeached of "high crimes and misdemeanors" on December 9, 1870. One of the charges was that Holden had misused his power as governor by ordering Kirk "and other evil disposed persons to assault, seize, detain, and imprison" free citizens of North Carolina. Kirk himself was placed under house arrest in Raleigh. With the aid of the Republican sheriff of Wake County, Kirk escaped, making his way back to Tennessee. For a time, Kirk worked in the U.S. Patent Office in Washington, D.C., and speculated in gold mining interests in the Allegheny Mountains. Eventually, he made his way to California. He was tormented by his past, believing that "the devil was coming for him." He even slept with a sword by his

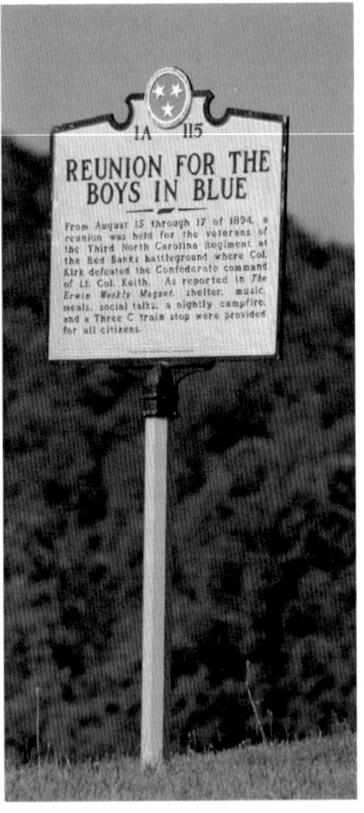

The members of Kirk's old regiment met at least once for a reunion, at the site of their victory over Confederates near Erwin, Tennessee. *Author's collection.*

side. George W. Kirk passed away in Gilroy, California, on February 15, 1905. He was sixty-eight years of age and buried in the Gavilan Hills Memorial Park in Santa Clara County, California.[232]

The vast majority of the rank and file, those trying to survive in the border counties, tried to get on with the rest of their lives. They married and raised families, adjusting to having family members who had served on opposite sides during the war. Some became the leaders of their communities, and a few served in higher offices. Others, like Stoneman and Kirk, headed west, looking for new adventures in Texas and California. From time to time, the old veterans got together to reminisce of the days gone by. Some of the North Carolina and Tennessee counties formed United Confederate Veterans Camps, inviting not only the boys in Gray but the boys in Blue as well to their annual reunions. The Thirteenth Tennessee Cavalry (U.S.) held several reunions in Tennessee. The Third North Carolina Mounted Infantry (U.S.) also held a reunion in February 1894. The veterans chose the site of the Battle of Red Banks, near Erwin, for their reunion.[233]

Slowly, the veterans and their families who bore witness to the war along the boundaries of North Carolina and Tennessee passed on. Some of them handed down stories to their sons and daughters and to their grandchildren, stories of a time when a simple knock at a door could bring a friend or a foe. The mountains themselves no longer bear witness to Kirk's War, and the animosities between families have settled. But for those who lived and endured those troubled years, and for those who died, their suffering will always serve as a testament to just how cruel humans can be to one another.

7

Looking for Kirk's War

There are many historic sites in the counties included in this study. Some, like Sycamore Shoals State Historic Site in Elizabethton, Tennessee, cover history prior to the war years, while others, like the Mineral Museum in Mitchell County, focus on issues after the war. There are several sites directly connected to the war itself.

North Carolina

Avery County. There are Civil War Trail markers in Cranberry (iron mines), Banner Elk (underground railroad for escaped prisoners) and between Linville and Montezuma (the Blalocks). The Banner House Museum, in Banner Elk, was constructed in 1865, just as the war was ending. It was the home of Samuel Banner, a veteran of the Fifth Ohio Infantry. The house was near the "Land of Goshen," a hiding area for dissidents and escaped prisoners trying to make their way to Federal lines.

Buncombe County. Vance Birthplace State Historic Site, near Weaverville, is a re-creation of the boyhood home of North Carolina's wartime governor. There are displays on his life and military service, along with a Civil War Trail marker. Buncombe County has ten other Civil War Trail markers. The markers at Ridgecrest and below Fairview on Alt-US 74 concern Stoneman's Raid, while a marker to the First United States Colored Heavy Artillery

Zebulon Baird Vance was born along Reams Creek in Buncombe County. His birthplace is now a North Carolina State Historic Site. *Author's collection.*

and its postwar garrison of Asheville is near the intersection of Broadway and Mount Clare Avenue. There are markers to Asheville's enslaved people (Charlotte Street); to Private George Avery, Fortieth United States Colored Troops (Dalton Street); and to Landsman Riley Powers, who served on the USS *Virginia* (Overlook Road). Two of the markers cover Asheville's defenses and the battle that took place there in April 1865 (Battery Potter, intersection of O. Henry Avenue and Battle Square, and Battle of Asheville, Campus Drive and Field Drive). The other markers are to Asheville's wartime prison (Montford Avenue and Hill Street) and the Smith-McDowell House, the 1840s brick home of a Confederate officer. Also in Asheville is Riverside Cemetery, the final resting place for Governor Zebulon Vance, his brother Robert Vance and Generals Thomas Clingman and James Green Martin. Major John W. Woodfin, killed in the October 1863 skirmish at Warm Springs, is also interred at Riverside. One other cemetery of note is the Academy Hill Cemetery. There are twenty-eight Confederate and five unknown Federal soldiers buried here. It is believed these men died in a local hospital during the war or shortly after its conclusion.

Haywood County. Waynesville has three Civil War Trail markers. Two of them concern the last days of the war in the area (Battle House on North

Main Street and Battle Engagement on Blink Bonny Drive). A third marker in Waynesville is for Greenhill Cemetery, the final resting place of Colonel William H. Thomas, commander of Thomas's Legion. In Maggie Valley is a marker with information on Kirk's February 1865 raid into the area, and in Canton is the Locust Field Cemetery marker, denoting a site for repeated Confederate rendezvous during the war. There is also a state historic marker in Waynesville marking the site of Martin's surrender.

Mars Hill College was destroyed during the war. It took years to rebuild. *Author's collection.*

MADISON COUNTY. There are Civil War Trail markers in Hot Springs (Warm Springs skirmish in 1863), Mars Hill (military activity at college) and Marshall (early war violence and salt raid). There is a state highway marker at the intersection of NC 208 and NC 212, near the site of the Shelton Laurel Massacre. In Marshall, there is the Colonel Lawrence Allen House, built in 1849.

WATAUGA COUNTY. There is a Civil War Trail marker at the old Cove Creek School (Camp Mast). There are also several highway markers denoting the role of Stoneman's men, including Kirk, in Deep Gap, Boone and Blowing Rock. The old Boone City Cemetery includes the graves of men killed during the March 1865 skirmish and members of the Second North Carolina Mounted Infantry who later died while occupying the town.

YANCEY COUNTY. In downtown Burnsville is a Civil War Trail marker noting the site of the April 1864 Burnsville Raid. Near the marker is the prewar home of John W. McElroy, Home Guard brigadier general. The home is now a part of the Rush-Wray Museum of Yancey County History.

The McElroy House was built for John W. McElroy, circa 1840. *Author's collection.*

Tennessee

Carter County. There are two Civil War Trail markers in Carter County. One is located at Roan Mountain State Park and provides information on the Carter family. The second is located in Elizabethton and features Samuel P. Carter, who was both a naval admiral and a general in the Union army. On the outskirts of Elizabethton is the Carter Mansion, built between 1775 and 1780. Daniel Ellis supposedly hid here once, trying to escape Confederates who were seeking Unionists. The house is now a part of Sycamore Shoals State Historic Site and is open for tours. Carter County also has state historic markers to Daniel Ellis, the "Old Red Fox"; Andrew Johnson's death; the Isaac Lincoln home, where Nancy Hanks Lincoln lived from 1808 to 1809; and General Samuel P. Carter.

The Carter Mansion, the oldest frame house in the state of Tennessee, bore witness to the tramp of soldiers' feet during the war. *Author's collection.*

Cocke County. Two Civil War Trail markers are in Parrottsville. The first details the hanging of Peter Reece, a local Unionist. It is located in the Parrott-LaRue-Myers Greenway and Recreational Park. The second marker (TN 340 and Old Highway 321) provides information on the slaves purchased in the area by future president Andrew Johnson.

Greene County. Greene County is an area rich in historic sites and markers. The Andrew Johnson National Historic Site in Greeneville contains several buildings once owned by the seventeenth president of the United States, including his tailor's shop. There is also a Civil War Trail marker at the site. Other Civil War Trail markers in Greeneville include Dickson-Williams Mansion (North Irish Street), where John Hunt Morgan spent his last night; hanging bridge burners at the old depot (Loretta Street); and Tusculum College (Shiloh Road). Two other markers are found in Mosheim. One is

A monument to the bridge burners was erected near the site of the Lick Creek Bridge in Greene County. *Author's collection.*

a marker for the Battle of Blue Springs (West Andrew Jackson Highway), and the other is for the Pottertown bridge burners (Pottertown Road). At the David Crockett Birthplace State Park in Limestone is a Civil War Trail marker that provides information on the area being a Unionist stronghold. There are nine Tennessee State Historic markers concerning Andrew Johnson, including one on his grave in Andrew Johnson National Cemetery. Other Tennessee State Historic markers include two markers for the Battle of Blue Springs; one on the bridge burners; Bull's Gap; death of John Hunt Morgan; and the Greeneville Union Conventions. The Greeneville/Greene County Museum (West McKee Street) has several exhibits on the Civil War in the area.

JOHNSON COUNTY. Mountain City, called Taylorsville during the war, has a Civil War Trail marker (West Main Street) that provides information on the struggle of local Southern sympathizers, outnumbered by their Unionist neighbors.

SEVIER COUNTY: A Civil War Trail marker in Sevierville (Old Newport Highway) marks the site of the Battle of Fair Oaks, fought in January 1864. Another Civil War Trail marker is located in Pigeon Forge (Old Mill Avenue) and provides information on the Sevier County Home Guard. In Gatlinburg are two Civil War Trail markers. The first is on Fort Harry (Cherokee Orchard Road), a fortification built by men from Thomas's Legion. Second is the Reagan House/Burg Hill marker (Cherokee Orchard Road), which deals with a skirmish in December 1863. Among the Tennessee State Historic markers are ones for John H. Reagan, Confederate postmaster general, born in Gatlinburg, and Confederate general John Porter McCowan, born near Sevierville in 1815.

UNICOI COUNTY. There are Tennessee State Historic Markers at the Bell Cemetery (Limestone Cove Massacre) and the Battle of Red Banks and reunion of the Third North Carolina Mounted (U.S.).

WASHINGTON COUNTY. During the war, Johnson City was known as Haynesville, in honor of local politician Landon Carter Haynes. Haynes was one of two Confederate senators from Tennessee. He lived in Knoxville during the war, then Wythville and Statesville, before moving to Memphis after the end of the war. His home survived the war and is now the Tipton-Haynes State Historic Site. There is a Civil War Trail marker and a Tennessee Highway marker at the site (South Roan Street, Johnson City). Among the Tennessee State Historic Markers are signs for the birthplace of Confederate general Alfred Eugene Jackson, the Battle of Limestone Station and Carter's Raid.

APPENDIX

THE ROLE OF AFRICAN AMERICANS IN THE BORDER WAR

Finding concrete information about the role of both slaves and free people of color who lived in the border states is a challenge. It must suffice to say that the war affected them just as much as it did the whites living in the area. It is also evident that they suffered at the hands of many. East Tennessee and portions of Western North Carolina were Unionist in sentiment but not abolitionist. It was recorded that one of the first actions of William Blalock after his release from the Confederate army in the spring of 1862 was beating and robbing a "colored man by the name of Losson Farr, taking an ass from him among other things." After Blalock was wounded in January 1865, one of Blalock's gang "threatened to kill one of [Caroll Moore's] negroes if he didn't show him where his [Moore's] horses were hid."[234]

There were 5,549 slaves in the twelve mountain counties in this study. There were also a limited number of free people of color in the mountain counties, including 240 in North Carolina. A few of these men did serve in the Confederate army. Brothers Franklin and William Henry Cousins were freedmen living in Watauga County in 1860. George Folk kidnapped the brothers and took them to Asheville to work as camp servants. However, former local representative Mark Holtzclaw wrote the governor on their behalf, and they were released. In September 1861, the brothers voluntarily joined Company B, Thirty-Seventh North Carolina Troops. Franklin was killed fighting at Second Manassas, and William Henry was captured on April 2, 1865. He survived the war, moved to Yancey County and married the widow of another Confederate veteran. Another African American who served was Marcus Young, a slave owned by Captain Creed Young. Marcus wrote in his pension application that he was a teamster for Captain Young, possibly traveling with the Sixteenth North Carolina Troops. He also hauled "salt, coffee, and other merchandise from South Carolina into North Carolina for the use of Southern Troops and for domestic use." Peter Hardin, a slave belonging to Jordin Hardin, worked at the Cranberry Iron Mines during the war. It was his job to haul the local iron ore to the rail head near Morganton. Yet another slave who was a teamster for the Confederate army was Robert Stover of Carter County. There are undoubtedly more whom time and history have forgotten.[235]

Many of the African Americans in the area made their way into one of two regiments: the First United States Colored Heavy Artillery or the Fortieth United States Colored Troops. It can be assumed that the majority of these soldiers were former slaves, although the forms that were completed when they enlisted did not ask that question. There were recruiting stations established in Knoxville and presumably in Greeneville as well. As soon as these black refugees arrived in town, recruiters were trying to convince them to join the army. At one point, Andrew Johnson was authorized to pay slaveholding Southern Unionists who allowed their slaves to enlist. The First United States Colored Heavy Artillery was organized in Knoxville between February and November 1864. Many of the black men captured by Kirk when he raided Camp Vance in June 1864 joined this regiment. The regiment did duty in East Tennessee, Western Virginia, North Alabama and Western North Carolina. In May 1865, the First moved into Asheville for garrison duty. Along the way, four members of the regiment raped a young white woman and nearly killed her aunt and uncle, who tried to prevent it. The four were tried, found guilty and then executed for the crime by their regiment shortly thereafter. The First was mustered out of service on March 31, 1866. The Fortieth United States Colored Troops was mustered into service on February 29, 1864. Like the First, the Fortieth spent most of its time guarding railroads in East Tennessee. This regiment was mustered out of service on April 25, 1866. Unfortunately, there are no modern histories of either regiment.[236]

Some slaves undoubtedly simply walked off their farms and toward East Tennessee. Others were liberated like those during Kirk's raid on Camp Vance. Some tried to tag along when Federal soldiers who had escaped from a prison passed through the mountains. Often, the soldiers refused to take the slaves with them, reasoning that the Home Guard was only looking for

Andrew Johnson's slaves are remembered with a marker in the town of Parrottsville, Tennessee. *Author's collection.*

the prisoners as part of their job. A missed slave would turn out a community in the pursuit. William Burson, an escaped Ohio soldier, was hiding out in the Trap Hill section of Wilkes County and was considering taking five black men with him. Burson was warned that if caught with the runaways, he would be hanged. He told his five eager companions of the dangers. "'Well, well,' they said, 'nebber mind us, massa, we'll come arter awhile.'" There were many instances when the slaves assisted the escaped prisoners, Confederate deserters and dissidents as they made their way across the mountains. At times, the slaves actually aided the raiders. When Kirk was raiding Camp Vance, Lawson Avery burned his master's barn before joining the group and heading back over the mountain, according to local stories.[237]

Slavery legally ended in Tennessee on February 22, 1865, when the state constitution was amended, declaring immediate emancipation of all slaves in the state. Slavery in North Carolina did not end until December 4, 1865, when the state ratified the Thirteenth Amendment.

Not all slaves escaped or betrayed their masters. In Greeneville, Andrew Johnson freed his slaves on August 8, 1863. The few he had owned continued to live with the family, traveling to Washington, D.C., when Johnson became vice president. Rumor has it that the Banner slaves remained with the largely pro-Union Banner family. That was most certainly the case with Done, the slave of Ermine Farthing in the Bethel community of Watauga County; he stayed with the Farthings the rest of his life and is buried close to the family. Peter Hardin continued to work at the Cranberry Iron Mines. He did not die until 1916 and is buried close by in Avery County.

The roles of African Americans in the mountains of North Carolina and Tennessee, the regiments they served in and their lives after the war ended are stories that still need to be explored.[238]

Notes

CMSR, RG109, NA: Compiled Military Service Records, Record Group, National Archives

DU: Special Collections, Perkins Library, Duke University

NCDAH: North Carolina Division of Archives and History

OR: *The War of the Rebellion: A Compilation of the Official Records of the Union and Confederate Armies*

SHC: Southern Historical Collection, University of North Carolina–Chapel Hill

Introduction

1. *The War of the Rebellion: A Compilation of the Official Records of the Union and Confederate Armies*, 128 vols. (Washington, D.C.: Government Printing Office, 1880–1901), vol. 31, part 3, 297. All citations refer to series 1, unless noted.
2. Daniel E. Sutherland, *A Savage Conflict: The Decisive Role of Guerrillas in the American Civil War* (Chapel Hill: University of North Carolina Press, 2009), xi; Noel Fisher, "Definitions of Victory: East Tennessee Unionists in the Civil War and Reconstruction," in *Guerrillas, Unionists, and Violence on the Confederate Home Front*, edited by Daniel E. Sutherland (Fayetteville: University of Arkansas Press, 1999), 97; Michael C. Hardy, *The Fifty-Eighth North Carolina Troops: Tar Heels in the Army of Northern Virginia*. (Jefferson, NC: McFarland and Company, 2010), 185–86.

Chapter 1

3. Calvin J. Cowles to "Uncle," June 17, 1861, Cowles Letter Book, NCDAH; *New Bern Daily Progress*, May 27, 1861.
4. Paul Fink, *Jonesborough: The First Century of Tennessee's First Town* (Johnson City, TN: Overmountain Press, 1989), 143; *Asheville News*, January 9, 1862.
5. *Tennessee State Gazetteer and Business Directory for 1860–1861* (Nashville, TN: John L. Mitchell, 1860), 76–77.
6. Henry Melville Doak Memoirs, typescript, Confederate Collection, Tennessee State Library and Archives, Nashville; *Asheville News*, November 1, 1861.
7. *Asheville News*, November 1, 1860.
8. *Asheville Spectator*, January 2, 1861; *Asheville News*, January 31, 1861; Samuel Deaver to Zebulon Vance, January 28, 1861, *Zebulon Baird Vance Letters*, vol. 1, edited by Frontis Johnston (Raleigh, NC, 1963), 91–92; *Semi-Weekly Standard*, January 10, 1861; John Inscoe and Gordon McKinney, *The Heart of Confederate Appalachia: Western North Carolina in the Civil War* (Chapel Hill: University of North Carolina Press, 2000), 46.
9. John B. Palmer to Andrew Johnson, August 25, 1865, Case Files of Applications from Former Confederates for Presidential Pardons, 1861–1867, RG 94, NA; *Fayetteville Semi-Weekly*, February 25, 1861.
10. *Raleigh Register*, March 13, 1861.
11. Oliver P. Temple, *East Tennessee and the Civil War* (Cincinnati, OH: Robert Clarks Company, 1899), 173–74; *Knoxville Whig*, January 19, 1861, February 2, 1861; Jeannette Greve, *The Story of Gatlinburg* (Gatlinburg, TN: Brazo Printing Company, 1976), 3–78; Charles Johnson to Andrew Johnson, January 1, 1861, *The Papers of Andrew Johnson*, 13 vols., edited by Leroy P. Graf, Ralph Haskins and Paul Bergeron (Knoxville: University of Tennessee Press, 1967), vol. 4, 110–111.
12. *Knoxville Whig*, February 16, 1861.
13. Nicholas Woodfin to Weldon Edwards, April 13, 1861, Conway Collection, NCDAH.
14. Wilson J. Brown to John E. Brown, April 15, 1861, Theodore Davidson Morrison Papers, SHC; Clement Dowd, *The Life of Zebulon B. Vance* (Charlotte, NC: Observer Printing and Publishing, 1897), 441; Francis Dedmond, ed., "Harvey Davis's Unpublished Civil War 'Diary' and the Story of Company D of the First North Carolina Cavalry," *Appalachian Journal* 13 (Summer 1986): 379.

15. *Knoxville Whig*, April 20, 1861; *The Tennessean*, April 5, 1861; Melanie Storie, *The Dreaded Thirteenth Tennessee Union Cavalry: Marauding Mountain Men* (Charleston, SC: The History Press, 2013), 20; Joyce Cox, ed., *History of Washington County, Tennessee* (Johnson City, TN: Overmountain Press, 2001), 177; *Knoxville Register*, May 24, 1861.
16. *Knoxville Whig*, May 25, June 1, 1861; Speech at Elizabethton, May 15, 1861, *The Papers of Andrew Johnson*, 4:477–78; *Jonesborough Express*, May 10, 17, 1861; W.H. Churchwell to Landon Carter Haynes, May 6, 1861, Nelson Papers, McClung Collection, Lawson McGee Library, Knoxville, Tennessee.
17. Noel Fisher, *War at Every Door: Partisan Politics and Guerrilla Violence in East Tennessee, 1860–1869* (Chapel Hill: University of North Carolina Press, 1997), 35.
18. *Knoxville Whig*, June 29, 1861; Temple, *East Tennessee*, 357–58.
19. *Jonesborough Union*, May 4, 1861.
20. Chapel Church, *Records Abstract, 1859–1904*, Ashe County Public Library.
21. *Daily Nashville Patriot*, August 25, 1861; Thomas Hume, *The Loyal Mountaineers of East Tennessee* (Knoxville, TN: Ogden Brothers and Company, 1888), 308; *OR* 4:251, 393; Fisher, *War at Every Door*, 42.
22. *Raleigh Register*, August 21, 1861; *Augusta (GA) Chronicle*, September 4, 1861; *Raleigh Standard*, September 14, 1861; Barzilla McBride to brother and sister, August 25, 1862, in possession of the author.
23. *OR* 2:69, 201.
24. Zollicoffer to Cooper, August 6, 1861, Orders and Letters Sent, Brigadier General Felix K. Zollicoffer, August 1861 to January 1861, RG109, NA.
25. *OR* 4:393, 399, 404; *Athens Post*, September 13, 1861.
26. *OR* 4:393.
27. Oliver Temple, *Notable Men of Tennessee from 1833 to 1875* (New York: Cosmopolitan Press, 1912), 90; David Madden, "Unionist Resistance to Confederate Occupation: The Bridge Burners of East Tennessee," *East Tennessee Historical Society's Publication* 52:25–27.
28. *OR* 4:317, 320.
29. Ibid., 487, 515.
30. Ibid., 300, 347.
31. Temple, *East Tennessee*, 382–83.
32. *OR* 4:862; Temple, *East Tennessee*, 385.
33. Temple, *East Tennessee*, 385.
34. *OR* 4:236; 7:701; *OR*, ser. 2, 1:842–43.
35. Danville Leadbetter, Special Order 216 (1), CMSR, RG109, NA; Cox, *Washington County*, 158; Daniel Ellis, *The Thrilling Adventures of Daniel*

Ellis (New York: Harper and Brothers, 1867), 29; *Memphis Daily Appeal*, November 29, 1861; *Nashville Union and American*, November 26, 1861.

36. *OR* 7:712–13; *Daily Nashville Patriot*, December 8, 1861; *Richmond Dispatch*, December 13, 1861.

37. *OR* 7:747–48; *OR*, ser. 2, 1:851.

38. *OR* 7:726; Temple, *East Tennessee*, 393, 401; *Daily Nashville Patriot*, December 14, 1861; William Brownlow, *Sketches of the Rise, Progress, and Decline of Secession* (Philadelphia: J.B. Lippincott, 1862), 319, 421; *OR*, ser. 2, 1:864–989.

39. Temple, *East Tennessee*, 399, 401; *Greeneville Sun*, May 12, 2006.

Chapter 2

40. *Wilmington Journal*, December 19, 1861; *Fayetteville Semi-Weekly Observer*, December 19, 1861.

41. Weymouth Jordan, Louis Manarin, et. al. *North Carolina Troops, 1861–1865: A Roster*, 20 vols. (Raleigh: North Carolina Division of Archives and History, 1961–present), 10:105, 14:274, 16:7 (hereafter cited as *NC Troops*); *Semi-Weekly Journal*, January 4, 1862.

42. Adjutant General to Palmer, January 14, 1862, Adjutant General Letterbook, NCDAH; Thomas to Clark, Governor's Papers, NCDAH.

43. *OR* 7:842, 849; Hans Trefousse, *Andrew Johnson: A Biography* (New York: W.W. Norton, 1989), 152–54.

44. Smith to wife, March 10, 11, 1862, Smith Papers, SHC; *OR*, vol. 10, pt. 2, 308–9, 320–21.

45. *North Carolina Argus*, April 1, 1862; *Asheville News*, March 27, 1862.

46. *OR*, vol. 10, pt. 2, 402.

47. Bennett Smith to wife, April 17, 1862, private collection; L.B. Headerick to Harris, March 18, 1862, Brownlow Papers, Tennessee State Archives.

48. Pension record of John W. Edwards, sent to the author by Tine Cole, January 27, 2008.

49. James Hodges to John Crawford, August 30, 1862; W.A. Wash to John Crawford, September 10, 1862; Crawford Letters, East Tennessee State University.

50. *OR*, vol. 10, pt. 2, 114, 454; Robert Johnson to Johnson, April 8, 1862, *Papers of Andrew Johnson*, 5:280–81; Sarah E. Thompson Papers, DU; John Andes and Will McTeer, *Loyal Mountain Troopers* (Maryville, TN: Blount County Genealogical Society, 1992), 21–25.

51. *OR*, vol. 10, pt. 2, 640–41; ser. 4, vol. 2, pt. 1, 367–71.
52. James Baggett, *Homegrown Yankees* (Baton Rouge: Louisiana State University Press, 2009), 26–27, 38, 51.
53. Shepherd Dugger, *War Trails of the Blue Ridge* (Banner Elk, NC: S.M. Dugger, 1932), 203; "The Banner Brothers of Co. B, 4th TN Cav (USA)," accessed February 15, 2002, http://www.rootsweb.com/~tncav/banner1.html.
54. W.M. Younce, *Adventures of a Conscript* (Cincinnati, OH: Editor Publishing, 1901), 5, 9, 15.
55. *Semi-Weekly Standard*, April 17, 1863; *Asheville News*, April 12, 1862, May 8, 1862; *Raleigh Register*, April 26, 1862.
56. *Asheville News*, April 24, 1862.
57. Ibid., May 8, 1862.
58. Ibid., June 26, 1862; *Raleigh Register*, October 29, 1862; *North Carolina Reports*, vol. 60 (Raleigh, NC: Edwards and Broughton Printing, 1917), 86–86.
59. *Spirit of the Age*, December 8, 1862; Rob Neufeld, "Murder of Sheriff in 1862," accessed January 16, 2017, http://thereadonwnc.ning.com/forum/topics/murder-of-sheriff-in-1862.
60. *Weekly Standard*, December 3, 1862; *Asheville News*, November 27, 1862; *Vance Papers* 1:399.
61. Noel Fisher, *The Civil War in the Smokies* (Gatlinburg, TN: Great Smoky Mountains Association, 2005), 62; *Asheville News*, July 3, 1862.
62. *OR*, vol. 16, pt. 2, 773–74.
63. *Jonesboro Express*, August 15, 1862; *Lynchburg Virginian*, October 3, 1862; *Nashville Daily Union*, October 15, 1862.
64. Younce, *Adventures of a Conscript*, 19–25.
65. R.A. Ragan, *Escape from East Tennessee* (Washington, D.C.: James H. Dony, 1910), 12–24.
66. Ellis, *Thrilling Adventures*, 57–75.

Chapter 3

67. Reeves to Vance, December 15, 1862, *Vance Papers*, 1:438.
68. Karen Clinard and Richard Russell, eds., *Fear in North Carolina: The Civil War Journals and Letters of the Henry Family* (Asheville, NC: Reminiscing Books, 2008), 112; Muriel Earley Sheppard, *Cabins in the Laurel* (Chapel Hill: University of North Carolina Press, 1935), 58.
69. *Semi-Weekly Standard*, April 17, 1863, January 16, 1863; *North Carolina Argus*, April 1, 1862.

70. *Semi-Weekly Standard*, April 17, 1863.
71. Ibid.; *Charlotte Democrat*, January 20, 1863; A.P. Gaston, *Partisan Campaigns of Col. Lawrence M. Allen*. (Raleigh, NC: Edwards and Broughton, 1894), 10; *Daily Progress*, January 19, 1863.
72. Adjutant General to McElroy, January 15, 1863, Adjutant General Letterbook, NCDAH; *Daily Progress*, January 19, 1863; Clinard and Russell, *Fear in North Carolina*, 128.
73. *OR*, vol. 20, pt. 2, 466.
74. *Chattanooga Daily Rebel*, February 8, 1863; *Daily Journal*, February 7, 1863; *Roan Mountain Republican*, October 7, 1876.
75. Ellis, *Thrilling Adventures*, 105–9.
76. Thomas to Mrs. Thomas, January 28, 1863, Thomas Collection, DU; "Record of Events," muster roll abstracts, January–February and March–April 1863, Company K, Infantry Regiment, Thomas's Legion, CMSR, RG109, NA.
77. *OR* 18:810.
78. Gaston, *Partisan Campaign*, 11–12; *Union Flag*, October 13, 1865; Phillip Paludan, *Victims: A True Story of the Civil War* (Knoxville: University of Tennessee Press, 1981), 98.
79. *OR*, ser. 2, vol. 5, 956; *NC Troops* 15:42–143.
80. *OR* 18:854; A.S. Merrimon to Vance, January 31, 1863, Vance to William Davis, *Vance Papers* 2:37, 41–42.
81. *OR* 18:881; Paludan, *Victims*, 104.
82. *Union Flag*, October 13, 1865; *New York Herald*, December 3, 1868; James Kirk, CMSR, Roll 74, M395, RG 94, NA; *Greensboro Patriot*, September 15, 1870.
83. *Greensboro Patriot*, September 15, 1870; George W. Kirk, CMSR, Roll 74, M396, RG94, NA. Vernon Crow writes that Kirk joined the Confederate army but quickly deserted in *Storm in the Mountains: Thomas' Confederate Legion of Cherokee Indians and Mountaineers* (Cherokee, NC: Press of the Museum of the Cherokee Indian, 1982), 104.
84. Ellis, *Thrilling Adventures*, 416–18; Stephen Thomas to Dr. Lillard, February 6, 1863, Lillard Family Papers, Tennessee State Library and Archives; William Penland to Dear Father, March 2, 1863, copy in author's possession.
85. Ellis, *Thrilling Adventures*, 147; Samuel Scott and Samuel Angel, *History of the Thirteenth Tennessee Cavalry* (Philadelphia: P.W. Ziegler and Company, 1973), 333; Crawford to Johnson, June 11, 1863, *Andrew Johnson Letters* 6:243; *Knoxville Register*, June 2, 1863.

86. *Abington Virginian*, July 17, 1863; Anna Mary Moon, "Civil War Memoirs of Mrs. Adeline Deaderick," *Tennessee Historical Quarterly* 7, no. 1 (March 1948): 54; *Greeneville Sun*, July 29, 1999; J. Metcalf to Vance, July 6, 1863, Vance Papers, NCDAH; R.V. Blackstock to Vance, July 24, 1863, Vance Papers, NCDAH.
87. *OR* 18:886–87; vol. 50, pt. 2, 709–710; Hardy, *The Fifty-Eighth North Carolina*, 80; James C. Taylor, "The 60th North Carolina Regiment: A Case Study of Enlistment and Desertion in Western North Carolina During the Civil War," master's thesis, Western Carolina University, 1996, 110.
88. *OR*, vol. 30, pt. 4, 560; W. Todd Groce, *Mountain Rebels: East Tennessee Confederates and the Civil War, 1860–1870* (Knoxville: University of Tennessee Press, 1999), 88–108.
89. Thomas L. Norwood to Uncle, June 16, 1863, Lenoir Papers, SHC; *NC Troops* 14:315; Hattie Lewis et al, *History of Cove Creek Baptist Church, 1799–1999* (Sugar Grove, NC: Cove Creek Baptist Church, 1999), 10.
90. W.A. Wash, *Camp, Field and Prison Life* (St. Louis, MO: Southwestern Book and Publishing, 1870), 20; Hardy, *Fifty-Eighth North Carolina Troops*, 59.
91. Gerald Cook, *The Last Tar Heel Militia, 1861–1865* (Winston-Salem, NC, 1987), 35.
92. Jos. C. Norwood to My Dear Walter, August 13, 1863, Lenoir Family Papers, SHC; John Arthur, *History of Watauga County* (Johnson City, TN: Overmountain Press, 1992), 170; *Historical Encyclopedia of Illinois*, vol. 3 (Chicago: Munsell Publishing, 1912), 1275.
93. Scott and Angel, *Thirteenth Tennessee*, 358–59; *Johnson Letters* 6:243; *Jonesborough Express*, August 28, 1863; Trefousse, *Andrew Johnson*, 162; *OR* ser. 4, vol. 3, 823.
94. Fisher, *War at Every Door*, 78–79.
95. Cox, *Washington County*, 196–97.
96. Ibid., 197–98.
97. McElroy to Vance, June 12, 1863, Governor's Papers, NCDAH; Fisher, *War at Every Door*, 134.
98. *NC Troops* 15:234–37; Joseph M. Squibb, CMSR, RG 94, Roll 149, NA; the information on the enlistees was gleaned from the compiled service records of the Second North Carolina Mounted Infantry, RG 94, rolls 014–018.
99. *OR* vol. 52, pt. 1, 473; James A. Smith, CMSR, RG 94, Roll 0018, NA.
100. Scott and Angel, *Thirteenth Tennessee*, 111; Storie, *Dreaded Thirteenth*, 48.

101. Survey of the Compiled Service Records, Thirteenth Tennessee Cavalry, RG 94, rolls 103–108, NA; Scott and Angel, *Thirteenth Tennessee*, 113; Storie, *Dreaded Thirteenth*, 48.
102. Gaston, *Col. Lawrence M. Allen*, 14; *Fayetteville Observer*, October 1, 1863; Lloyd Bailey, *The Heritage of the Toe River Valley*, vol. 8 (Marceline, MO: Walsworth Publishing, 2009), 48.
103. *OR* vol. 31, pt. 1, 15; Sadie Smathers Patton, *Foundation Stones of Madison County* (N.p., 1951), 86.
104. *Madison County Heritage*, vol. 1 (Waynesville, NC: Don Mills, 1994), 435; Gaston, *Col. Lawrence M. Allen*, 14; *Greensboro Patriot*, November 5, 1863; Clinard and Russell, *Fear in North Carolina*, 168; Patton, *Foundation Stones of Madison County*, 86.
105. *Charlotte Democrat*, December 1, 1863; Gaston, *Col. Lawrence M. Allen*, 14–15.
106. *Charlotte Democrat*, December 1, 1863; Gaston, *Col. Lawrence M. Allen*, 160; Bailey, *Toe River Heritage* 8:46, 47.
107. *Fayetteville Semi-Weekly Observer*, November 9, 1863.
108. Survey of 2nd NCMI Compiled Service Records.
109. *OR* vol. 29, pt. 2, 837.
110. Susan Blackford, *Letters from Lee's Army* (New York: Scribner's Sons, 1947), 226.
111. R.T. Coles, *From Huntsville to Appomattox* (Knoxville: University of Tennessee Press, 1996), 153; James Faust, *The Fighting Fifteenth Alabama* (Jefferson, NC: McFarland and Company, 2014), 105; Thomas Hickerson, *Echoes of Happy Valley* (Chapel Hill, NC, 1962), 101; Calvin Cowles to Governor Zebulon Vance, April 4, 1864, Calvin Cowles Papers, NCDAH; *NC Troops* 16:145–46.
112. *Weekly State Journal*, January 19, 1864; Ellis, *Thrilling Adventures*, 328–29.
113. Ellis, *Thrilling Adventures*, 329; *Congressional Serial Set*, 360; 1860 U.S. Federal Census, Slave Schedule, Carter County, Tennessee.
114. Ellis, *Thrilling Adventures*, 329–30; *Reports of Committees of the Senate of the United States for the First Session of the Forty-Ninth Congress, 1885–1886*, vol. 10, 305–6; Fay Byrd, *Wilkes County Bits and Pieces* (Charleston, SC: Lulu, 2011), 219.
115. Ellis, *Thrilling Adventures*, 331; *Brownlow's Knoxville Whig*, April 16, 1864; Byrd, *Wilkes County Bits*, 219.
116. Samuel Cooper to Zebulon Vance, December 4, 1864, Governor's Papers, NCDAH; *OR* vol. 31, pt. 1, 439–40; Charles Kirk, *History of the Fifteenth Pennsylvania Cavalry* (Philadelphia, 1906), 333; *Charlotte Democrat*, January 26, 1864.
117. *Greensboro Patriot*, January 7, 1864.

Chapter 4

118. Hardy, *Fifty-Eighth North Carolina*, 85–93.
119. *OR* vol. 32, pt. 2, 30.
120. Ibid., pt. 1, 75–76.
121. *Daily Confederate*, May 17, 1864; Crow, *Storm in the Mountains*, 56.
122. James R. Love to Samuel Cooper, February 15, 1864, William Walker CMSP, reel 574, RG10, NA; *NC Troops* 16:147; Ellis, *Thrilling Adventures*, 208–12; *Memphis Daily Appeal*, January 21, 1864.
123. *OR*, vol. 32, pt. 1, 24–25; Fisher, *Civil War in the Smokies*, 129.
124. *OR*, vol. 32, pt. 2, 611.
125. Ibid., pt. 1, 137; W.L. Sanford, *History of the Fourteenth Illinois Cavalry* (Chicago: R.R. Donnelley, 1898), 143–52; L.F. Siler to Governor Vance, February 8, 1864, Governor Vance Papers, NCDAH; *Western Democrat*, March 1, 1864.
126. *Semi-Weekly Standard*, February 9, 1864; *Daily Progress*, March 30, 1864; Walter Clark, ed., *Histories of the Several Regiments and Battalions from North Carolina in the Great War 1861–1865*, 5 vols. (Goldsboro, NC: Nash Brothers Book and Job Printers, 1901), vol. 3, 666–67 (hereafter cited as Clark, *NC Regiments*); Colonel Allen's memoirs mention a skirmish between Allen and Kirk on February 20, 1864. There is, however, no consensus that Allen was even in North Carolina at the time. See *NC Troops* 15:155–56, n47, n49; Gaston, *Col. Lawrence M. Allen*, 16–17.
127. Kirk, George W., Eighth Tennessee Cavalry (US) CMSR, M395, Roll 74, RG94; SO #44, George W. Kirk, Third North Carolina Mounted Infantry, CMSR, M401, Roll 21, RG94, NA. Schofield also referred to Kirk as a major of the Second North Carolina Mounted Infantry, but there is no record of Kirk ever being mustered into that regiment.
128. Charles Wilson to J.A. Campbell, April 14, 1864, George W. Kirk CMSR, Roll 21, M401, RG94, NA; *OR*, vol. 32, pt. 3, 74.
129. *Weekly Progress*, March 13, 1864.
130. *Daily Progress*, March 30, 1864; John Bennett, CMSR, Roll 103, M395, RG94, NA; *NC Troops* 15:157; Eben Childs to Zebulon Vance, April 18, 1864, Governor's Papers, NCDAH.
131. *OR* 18:810; Robert V. Blackstock to Vance, April 18, 1864, Governor's Papers, NCDAH.
132. James M. Ray to Vance, April 22, 1864, Governor's Papers, NCDAH.
133. *OR* 18:810; Robert V. Blackstock to Vance, April 29, 1864, Governor's Papers, NCDAH; *Asheville News*, April 21, 1864.

134. *Daily Progress*, April 22, 1864; *Charlotte Democrat*, April 26, 1864; *Vance Letters* 3:181.
135. *OR* (Supplement) 6:236, 15:321, 30:234–35; Stringfield, Diary, April 26, 1864, and Stringfield to Sister Mollie, April 30, 1864, Stringfield Papers, NCDAH.
136. *OR* (Supplement) 15:231, 30:228, 235, 244.
137. *Charlotte Democrat*, May 10, 1864.
138. Ibid., June 14, 1864; Fisher, *Civil War in the Smokies*, 88–89; Bailey, *Heritage of the Toe River Valley*, 8:64; H.B. Roberts, *Olden Times in Greene County* (N.p.: H.B. Roberts, 1983), 1:81.
139. Fisher, *Civil War in the Smokies*, 67–68.
140. *OR*, vol. 39, pt. 2, 72–73.
141. Willis Perry Rogers, 2nd NCMI, CSR, M401, Roll0012, RG94; J.V. Franklin to John P. Arthur, March 2, 1912, quoted in Arthur, *Western North Carolina*, 606. Using the same quoted passage, Barrett believes the liberation of prisoners at Salisbury was the primary mission of the raid. The possibility of releasing the prisoners, however, does not appear in any of the period literature. John Barrett, *The Civil War in North Carolina* (Chapel Hill: University of North Carolina Press, 1963), 235.
142. Thompson to Cate, August 21, 1863, quoted in Walter Hilderman, *They Went into the Fight Cheering: Confederate Conscription in North Carolina* (Boone, NC: Parkway Publishers, 2006), 140.
143. Greg Mast, ed., "The Setser Letters," pt. 4, *Company Front* (August–September 1989), 14–15.
144. *Philadelphia Inquirer*, July 22, 1864; John Arthur, *Western North Carolina: A History* (Raleigh, NC: Edwards and Broughton, 1914), 605; Fisher, *Civil War in the Smokies*, 75–76; George W. Kirk obituary newspaper clipping, John Anderson Fain Collection, vol. 5, Box 3, East Tennessee State University. The *Philadelphia Inquirer* reported sixteen Confederate dead with eight prisoners and one Federal wounded.
145. Arthur, *Western North Carolina*, 605–6; *Army Mail Bag*, July 12, 1864; *News-Herald*, March 23, 1905; Eugene Willard, ed., *A Standard History of the Hanging Rock Region of Ohio*, 2 vols. (N.p.: Lewis Publishing, 1916), 2:656–57; *Carolina Watchman*, July 4, 1864.
146. *Carolina Watchman*, July 11, 1864.
147. Henry Castle, *History of St. Paul and Vicinity*, 3 vols. (Chicago: Lewis Publishing Company, 1912), 3:1080. Some later accounts state that there was a skirmish among the rows of huts at Camp Vance. For references to the skirmish, see Derald Hendry, *Burke County Facts and Folklore* (N.p., 1985), 40–41.

148. *NC Troops* 17:29, 144; *Charlotte News*, September 26, 1920; *OR*, vol. 39, pt. 1, 237. According to volume 20 of the *NC Troops*, 101 men captured at Camp Vance were imprisoned. Of these, 44 died of disease and 10 joined the Federal army.
149. *Daily Progress*, July 6, 1864; *Andrew Johnson Papers* 7:19.
150. *Charlotte News*, July 22, 1905; *News-Herald*, March 23, 1905.
151. *OR*, vol. 39, pt. 1, 237; Castle, *History of St. Paul and Vicinity* 3:1084; *Daily Progress*, July 6, 1864; *Carolina Watchman*, July 4, 1864; *Charlotte News*, July 22, 1905.
152. *Daily Watchman*, July 2, 1864; *Daily Progress*, July 6, 1864; Shepherd Dugger, *War Trails of the Blue Ridge*, 129–30; George Hahn, *The Catawba Soldiers of the Civil War* (Hickory, NC: Clay Print Company, 1911), 343.
153. Horton Cooper, *History of Avery County* (N.p., 1964), 35–36; Arizona Hughes, *Aunt Zona's Web* (Banner Elk, NC: Puddingstone Press, 1976), 4–5; Dugger, *War Trails of the Blue Ridge*, 131–33.
154. *Charlotte Democrat*, August 13, 1867; *Greensboro Patriot*, September 15, 1870.
155. *Army Mail Bag*, July 18, 1864; *OR*, vol. 39, pt. 1, 232–33; *Philadelphia Inquirer*, July 33, 1864; *New York Times*, July 10, 1864; *Daily Ohio Statesman*, July 11, 1864.
156. *OR*, vol. 39, pt. 1, 235–36; *Daily Progress*, July 6, 1864.
157. *Semi-Weekly Standard*, July 15, 1864; Matthew Bumgarner, *Kirk's Raiders* (Hickory, NC: Piedmont Press, 2000), 48.
158. Memoirs of William Gibbs Allen, Tennessee State Library; L. Cowles to Mary, July 24, 1864, Cowles Family Papers, North Carolina State Archives; *Charlotte Democrat*, July 5, 1864; *Daily Confederate*, July 2, 1864.
159. *OR*, vol. 39, pt. 2, 657; James Ramage, *Rebel Raider: The Life of General John Hunt Morgan* (Lexington: University of Kentucky Press, 1995), 228–29; Fisher, *War at Every Door*, 118; Ellis, *Thrilling Adventures*, 286.
160. Michael C. Hardy, *The Thirty-Seventh North Carolina Troops: Tar Heels in the Army of Northern Virginia* (Jefferson, NC: McFarland, 2009), 236; *Daily Progress*, August 23, 1864; Ellis, *Thrilling Adventures*, 281, 282–85. There was only one soldier with the last name Teener in the Confederate army.
161. "Adjutant General" to "Commanding Officer 68th N.C.T.," July [21?] 1864, Adjutant Generals Letter Book, AG-55, NCDAH.
162. Clark, *NC Regiments* 3:719.
163. *Daily Progress*, August 14, 1864.
164. Ezekiel Kirkendall, CMSR, Roll 16, M401, RG94, NA; William Gentry, Case Files of Approved Pension Applications of Widows and other Veterans, RG15, NA.

165. Francis Hosmer, *A Glimpse of Andersonville and Other Writings* (Springfield, MA: Loring and Axtell, 1896), 15–23.
166. Moon, "Civil War Memoirs of Mrs. Adeline Deaderick," 57; Arthur, *Watauga County*, 172–73.
167. Storie, *Dreaded Thirteenth*, 54–62; *OR*, vol. 39, pt. 2, 75–76.
168. Storie, *Dreaded Thirteenth*, 64–66; Morgan, *Rebel Raider*, 227–29; "Sarah Thompson's Account of Morgan's Defeat," Sarah E. Thompson Papers, 1859–1898, Special Collections, DU.
169. Vaughn to D.M. Key, September 28, 1864, David Key Papers, SHC; *OR*, vol. 43, pt. 2, 866.
170. George W. Kirk, CMSR, M401, Roll0021, RG94. NA; *OR*, vol. 39, pt. 3, 571.
171. Scott and Angel, *Thirteenth Tennessee Cavalry*, 154. A different version appears in the pension application of Robert McCall's widow. Gillem testified that McCall and the two others were sent out to find General Burbridge in an effort to coordinate an attack on the salt works in Virginia. See Robert B. McCall, Civil War Widows Pension File, RG15, NA.
172. *OR*, vol. 39, pt. 3, 819; Larry Gordon, *The Last Confederate General: John C. Vaughn and His East Tennessee Cavalry.* (Minneapolis, MN: Zenith Press, 2009), 125–29.
173. *Brownlow's Knoxville Whig and Rebel Ventilator*, November 2, 1864.
174. *OR*, vol. 39, pt. 1, 852–54; Gordon, *Last Confederate General*, 129–31.
175. Storie, *Dreaded Thirteenth*, 72–82; Gordon, *Last Confederate General*, 129–33.
176. Paludan, *Victims*, 22; Larry Lemasters and Paul Whitman, "Die Like a Damned Dog," *Civil War Times Illustrated* 38, no. 4 (August 1999): 60–68; Manly Wellman, *The Kingdom of Madison: A Southern Mountain Fastness and Its People* (Chapel Hill: University of North Carolina Press, 1973), 88–89.
177. *North Carolina Argus*, September 22, 1864; Kristin Whitson, *Red Hill: The Untold Story of the Whitson Brothers and the Murder of Kit Byrd* (Clinton, TN: K.B and S.R. Whitson, 2007), 21.
178. Scott and Angel, *Thirteenth Tennessee Cavalry*, 352–53; *OR*, vol. 39, pt. 3, 813–14; Blackstock to Vance, October 21, 1864, Governor's Papers, NCDAH; *Daily Progress*, November 1, 1864; Bailey, *Heritage of the Toe River Valley* 8:64–69.
179. *OR*, vol. 42, pt. 3, 1279, 53:380–81.
180. Ibid., vol. 45, pt. 2, 54; Stephen Star, *The Union Cavalry in the Civil War*, 3 vols. (Baton Rouge: Louisiana State University Press, 2007), 3:80.
181. *OR*, vol. 45, pt. 1, 810–11; *Fayetteville Weekly Observer*, January 30, 1865.

182. A. Christine Tipton, *Civil War in the Mountains: Greasy Cove, Tennessee* (Erwin, TN: Shining Mountain Publishers, 2000), 15, 20–25; *OR*, vol. 45, pt. 1, 842; *OR*, vol. 45, pt. 2, 609; Bumgarner, *Kirk's Raiders*, 148–52.
183. *OR*, vol. 45, pt. 1, 842.

Chapter 5

184. William Burson, *A Race for Liberty* (Wellsville, OH: O.W.G. Foster, 1867), 103–4; Dugger, *War Trails of the Blue Ridge*, 113–17; Arthur, *Watauga County*, 174; *Weekly Standard*, November 23, 1864; *Public Laws in North Carolina*, Adjourned Session (1865), 65.
185. *NC Troops* 7:535; Arthur, *Watauga County*, 160; *Western Democrat*, May 6, 1862.
186. Arthur, *Watauga County*, 160–66.
187. William Blalock affidavit, November 3, 1874, Blalock Pension Application, NA; Arthur, *Watauga County*, 161.
188. *Congressional Record*, vol. 169 (1886): 169.
189. Mrs. McCaleb Coffey to John Benton, October 24, 1878, Pension Application.
190. *OR*, vol. 45, pt. 2, 621; Catherin Ray Pension Application, #128420, RG15, NA; Milton Henson, CMSR, Roll 21, M401, RG 94, NA; Clark, *NC Regiments* 3:758.
191. *Charlotte Democrat*, March 21, 1865; W. Clark Medford, *The Early History of Haywood County* (Waynesville, NC: Medford, 1961), 138.
192. Curtis Wood Jr., *Haywood County: Portrait of a Mountain Community* (Waynesville, NC: Historical Society of Haywood County, 2009), 69–70, 182; Hattie Davis, *Reflections of Cataloochie Valley and Its Vanished People from the Great Smoky Mountains* (Maggie Valley, TN: H.C. Press, 1999), 72–73; Fisher, *Civil War in the Smokies*, 137.
193. *Charlotte Democrat*, February 7, 1865; *Daily Progress*, February 9, 1865; *OR*, vol. 49, pt. 1, 1034–35; *NC Troops* 15:560–61.
194. I.N. Carr, "Mars Hill College in the War Between the States" (Military Collection, Box 76, Folder 76, NCDAH), 5–6; George W. Kirk, CMSR, M401, Roll0021; RG94, NA; *NC Troops* 8:265.
195. Crow, *Storm in the Mountains*, 118; Stringfield to Thomas, February 22, 1865, Thomas Papers, DU.
196. Arthur, *Watauga County*, 174–77, 283–84; Dugger, *War Trails of the Blue Ridge*, 118–19.
197. *OR*, vol. 49, pt. 1, 616, 663.

198. Ibid., vol. 47, pt. 2, 795, vol. 49, pt. 1, 916.

199. H.K. Weand, "Our Last Campaign and Pursuit of Jeff Davis," *History of the Fifteenth Pennsylvania Volunteer Cavalry* (Philadelphia: Society of the Fifteenth Pennsylvania Cavalry, 1906), 493; Chris Hartley, *Stoneman's Raid* (Winston-Salem, NC: John F. Blair, 2010), 62.

200. Finley Curtis Jr., "Stoneman Helps Himself," *Confederate Veteran* 27, no. 2 (May 1999): 182–85.

201. Roberts, *Olden Times in Greene County* 1:28; Fink, *Jonesborough*, 153; Fisher, *Civil War in the Smokies*, 87; Bailey, *Heritage of the Toe River Valley* 8:63; *Unicoi County Heritage*, 162; Sanna Gaffney, *Heritage of Watauga County, North Carolina*, vol. 1 (Winston-Salem, NC: Hunter Publishing Company, 1984), 373.

202. Roberts, *Olden Times in Greene County* 1:99; Fisher, *Civil War in the Smokies*, 89; Cranberry, *Historic Sites in Blount, Cocke, Monroe and Sevier Counties*; Gaffney, *Watauga County Heritage*, 373.

203. Fisher, *Civil War in the Smokies*, 89; *Watauga Democrat*, October 10, 1974.

204. Arthur, *Watauga County*, 178.

205. *NC Troops* 14:388; Arthur, *Watauga County*, 177; Cornella Spencer, *The Last Ninety Days of the War in North Carolina* (New York: Watchman Publishing, 1866), 193–94.

206. Ellis, *Thrilling Adventures*, 390–93; William C. Davis, ed., *Bluegrass Confederates: The Headquarters Diary of Edward O. Guettant* (Baton Rouge: Louisiana State University Press, 2005), 670; Isaac Bowers, CMSR, R333, M268, RG109, NA.

207. John Horton, Southern Claims Commission Approved Claims, 1871–1880, RG 217, NA; Arthur, *Watauga County*, 179; Barry Buxton, *A Village Tapestry: The History of Blowing Rock* (Boone, NC: Appalachian Consortium Press, 1989), 3.

208. Texle Barlow, *The Horton Family in Western North Carolina* (N.p.: n.d.), 53; Bud Altmayer, *As I Recall Old Blowing Rock, North Carolina* (Johnson City, TN: Overmountain Press, 1991), 63; Rittenhouse Baird, Joshua Winkler, William Vandyke and John Horton, Southern Claims Commission Approved Claims, 1871–1880, RG 217, NA; *Watauga Democrat*, December 30, 1928.

209. Bailey, *Heritage of the Toe River Valley* 8:51, 59–60; Samuel Honeycutt Southern Claims Commission Approved Claims, 1871–1880, RG 127, NA.

210. *Charlotte Observer*, December 22, 1895; *Lenoir Topic*, December 17, 1890, January 14, 1891; Spencer, *Last Ninety Days*, 195.

211. *OR*, vol. 49, pt. 1, 335–36.

212. Ibid., 31; Lewis Day, *Story of the One Hundred and First Ohio Infantry* (Cleveland, OH: W.M. Bayne Printing, 1894), 324; Clinard and Russell, *Fear in North Carolina*, 194.
213. *OR*, vol. 49, pt. 1, 28, 31; Clark, *NC Regiments* 3:669.
214. Clark, *NC Regiments* 3:669; Sondley, *History of Buncombe County*, 695; Day, *Story of the One Hundred and First Ohio Infantry*, 324–26; *OR*, vol. 49, pt. 1, 33; Clinard and Russell, *Fear in North Carolina*, 269.
215. Hartley, *Stoneman's Raid*, 352.
216. Milton Ready, *Asheville, Land of the Sky: An Illustrated History* (Northridge, CA: Windsor Publications, 1986), 27; Hartley, *Stoneman's Raid*, 353; Scott and Angel, *Thirteenth Tennessee Cavalry*, 240–41.
217. Hartley, *Stoneman's Raid*, 356–57.
218. Conley, "The Last Gun of the War," *Atlanta Constitution*, July 13, 1892; Clark, *NC Regiment* 3:760–61, 5:653, 655.
219. Stringfield, "Memoirs of the Civil War," typescript, McClung Collection, L-McGL.
220. *OR*, vol. 49, pt. 1, 550; Bumgarner, *Kirk's Raiders*, 73; Ellis, *Thrilling Adventures*, 360–61, 430.
221. Baggett, *Homegrown Yankees*, 338.

Chapter 6

222. Moon, "Civil War Memoirs of Mrs. Adeline Deaderick," 60, 61, 63.
223. Michael C. Hardy, *Watauga County, North Carolina in the Civil War* (Charleston, SC: The History Press, 2013), 80.
224. Fisher, *Civil War in the Smokies*, 144; Stringfield, "Memoirs of the Civil War," 14; Fisher, *War at Every Door*, 157.
225. Davis, *Civil War Letters and Memories from the Great Smoky Mountains*, 138.
226. *Charlotte Democrat*, December 17, 1865; *Raleigh Sentinel*, June 22, 1866; Groce, *Mountain Rebels*, 136–37, 139.
227. William C. Davis, ed., *The Confederate Generals*, 6 vols. (N.p.: National Historical Society, 1991), 6:69.
228. Gordon McKinney, *Zeb Vance: North Carolina's Civil War Governor and Gilded Age Political Leader* (Chapel Hill: University of North Carolina Press, 2013), 208 405.
229. Davis, *Confederate Generals* 2:160–61.
230. Ben Fordney, *George Stoneman: A Biography of the Union General* (Jefferson, NC: McFarland and Company, 2007), 122–56.

231. Ellis, *Thrilling Adventures*, 75, 103, 106, 122, 227; Daniel Ellis, Southern Claims–Barred and Disallowed, M1407, NA.

232. *Brownlow's Knoxville Whig*, March 27, 1867, May 8, 1867; William Powell, *North Carolina Through Four Centuries* (Chapel Hill: University of North Carolina Press, 1989), 399–403; Bumgarner, *Kirk's Raiders*, 97–102.

233. There were United Confederate Veterans Camps in Boone (Nimrod Triplett Camp 1273), Burnsville (General William D. Pender Camp 1154), Waynesville (Pink Welch Camp 548) and Johnson City (General John B. Gordon Camp 1400). There were Grand Army of the Republic Posts in Marshall (G.W. Gehagam Post 38), Greeneville (Burnside Post 8 and William Jackson Post 27), Romeo (Alfred Couch Post 24), Caney Branch (John F. Stum Post 48), Mosheim (John Baughart Post 51), Warrensburg (Byrd's Hill Post 52), Chucky City (Chucky City Post 83), Jeroldstown (Holtsinger Post 90), Johnson City (S.K.N. Patten Post 26), Jonesboro (Jonesboro Post 35), Elizabethton (P.P.C. Nelson Post 37), Newport (Newport Post 71), Butler (T.C. White Post 68) and Sevierville (A.C. Catlett Post 58).

Appendix

234. Carroll Moore affidavit, Wm. Blalock Pension application [083], NA.

235. Sometimes the last name is spelled Cozzens. For more details, see Hardy, *Watauga County in the Civil War*, 15–17, 80; Bailey, *Heritage of the Toe River Valley* 8:174.

236. *OR*, vol. 49, pt. 2, 670.

237. Burson, *Race for Liberty*, 79–82; Inscoe and McKinney, *Heart of Confederate Appalachia*, 229–30.

238. See John Inscoe, *Appalachians and Race: The Mountain South from Slavery to Segregation* (Lexington: University Press of Kentucky, 2005).

Index

I

J

K

L

M

N

P

Q

S

T

U

V

W

Y

About the Author

Michael C. Hardy's ancestors first moved to the Southern Appalachian Mountains in the mid-1700s. Some settled in Wilkes and Surry Counties and fought with the Overmountain Men at the Battle of Kings Mountain in 1780. Others lived in southwestern Virginia, eastern Kentucky and even eastern Tennessee. Michael's grandmother lived on Stoney Creek in Carter County during World War II, working in the war effort in Elizabethton. Michael moved to the mountains in 1995, living in both Watauga and Avery Counties. He is a graduate of the University of Alabama and the 2010 North Carolina Historian of the Year. Michael has authored twenty-two other books, and his articles have appeared in *Civil War Times*, *America's Civil War*, *North & South*, *Gettysburg Magazine*, *Tar Heel Junior Historians* and *Confederate Veteran.* Since 2014, he has reviewed books for *Blue and Gray* magazine. Michael is also the past chair of the Yancey Historical Association and of the Avery County Historical Society and Museum.

For two decades, Michael has volunteered at various historic sites in the area, including Sycamore Shoals State Park (Carter County) and the Tipton-Haynes State Historic Site (Johnson County) in Tennessee; Fort Defiance (Caldwell County), the Historic Carson House and the Mountain Gateway

Museum (McDowell County), the Smith-McDowell House and the Zebulon Baird Vance State Historic Site (Buncombe County). Since 2011, he has been a Volunteer-in-Parks on the Blue Ridge Parkway, providing historic interpretation about the Civil War in the mountains. In 2015, the Hardy family was named as volunteers of the year for the Pisgah District, Blue Ridge Parkway.

Michael lives in the Blue Ridge Mountains with his wife, Elizabeth, and children, Nathaniel and Isabella. When not volunteering, they enjoy hiking and exploring historic sites. You can learn more through his blog, Looking for North Carolina's Civil War, or his web page, www.michaelchardy.com.